LIFE AND TIMES OF A WAYWARD GEOLOGIST

A lifetime of personal anecdotes, adventures, and more...

John Craig Shaw

authorHOUSE®

AuthorHouse™
1663 Liberty Drive
Bloomington, IN 47403
www.authorhouse.com
Phone: 1 (800) 839-8640

First published by AuthorHouse   06/22/2011

ISBN: 978-1-4567-6980-2 (sc)
ISBN: 978-1-4567-6979-6 (hc)
ISBN: 978-1-4634-0246-4 (e)

Library of Congress Control Number: 2011908329

Print information available on the last page.

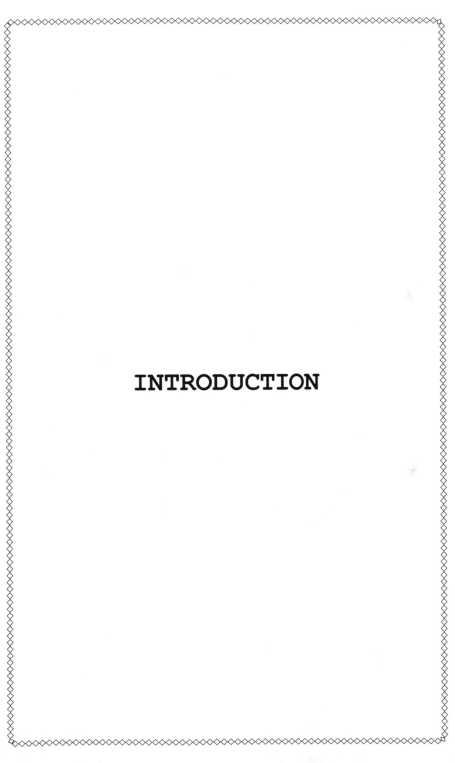

INTRODUCTION

This book is a collection of stories and anecdotes from the course of my life. Most of the book is in chronological order: my early life, school days, college, professional career and retirement. It is by no means a complete autobiography but I have included many true stories that I hope will be of interest to many readers--especially geologists, Corps of Engineers personnel and people who came of age during the volatile '60s and '70s.

I hope that the racial issues in some of the chapters do not offend readers. Being a few years older than the "Baby Boomer" generation, I was a college student at the University of Alabama during the midst of the historical "Civil Rights Era", when George Wallace "stood in the door". Several stories reflect those trying times. Fortunately, we have witnessed a change for the better in the South with regard to race relations.

My professional career as a geologist with the Mobile District Corps of Engineers was a challenge that sent me to several foreign countries and also on interesting assignments within the U.S. I spent 10 years as a field geologist, working with core drill crews on the early exploration and geological testing for the Tennessee-Tombigbee Waterway.

Another interesting assignment was work in Saudi Arabia, where I had many comical and hair-raising experiences.

This book is divided into six sections: Early Life, College Life, Graduate School, Professional Career, Retirement, and Miscellaneous. Some of the names and sequences of events may not be entirely accurate but I have written it down to the best of my memory.

Hopefully, this book will refresh older readers' memories of times gone by and bring a smile to others as they read the following stories.

John Craig Shaw

Contents

GRADUATE SCHOOL: UNIVERSITY OF HAWAII

PROFESSIONAL CAREER

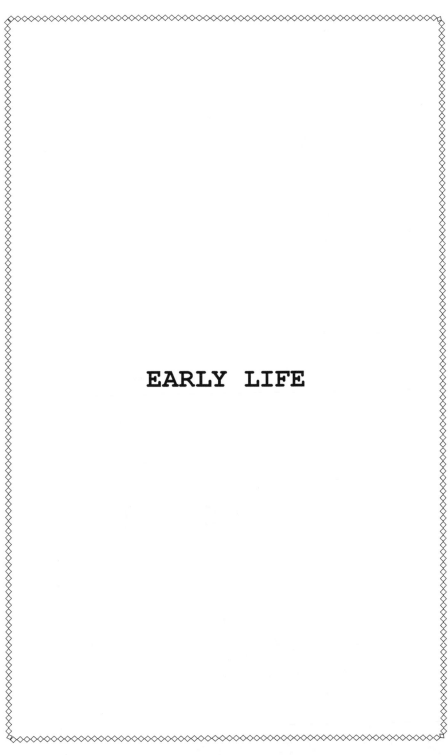

EARLY LIFE

Chapter 1

RHEA STREET GANG

Part 1

Some of the "Rhea St. Gang"
Author second from left

I was born March 6, 1943 at the Naval Hospital on North Island (Coronado), which is in San Diego County, California. My father, John Francis Shaw, was in the US Navy during the war, serving on mine sweeper and sub chaser vessels. He was a sonar operator. My mother, Jane Mobley Shaw, was a native of Amarillo, Texas. Both parents were artists and met at the Ringling School of Art in Sarasota, Florida.

A year or so after I was born, my father was relieved of his sea duty with the Navy because of stomach ulcers and chronic seasickness. He was transferred to the Naval Air Corps in Phoenix, Arizona where my parents rented a duplex in a grapefruit orchard. During this time, my father drew a regular comic strip for a U.S. Navy paper.

Just before the war ended, my mother and I went back to San Diego to stay with my grand parents while my sister Suzanne was born. On August 31, 1945, Suzanne was born in the City Hospital. She was actually delivered in the hospital cafeteria because of a shortage of rooms and doctors. At the time, injured Iwo Jima soldiers took priority.

When my father was discharged, he took the family back to his home state of Alabama. He was from Uniontown, Alabama, but we located in Mobile where he had a relative in the Juke Box rental business (Fox Automatic Music Co.).
A large post-war subdivision (Westlawn) had just been built on the western edge of the city, and we eventually bought a house on Rhea Avenue. At this time my father went into Civil Service work at Brookley Air Force Base, packing parachutes. My mother wanted to offer private art lessons to children, so in about 1949(?) an art studio was built out of crossties, in the back yard. My

mother taught children's art lessons to at least two generations. Many former students are now well known artists, as well as professionals in all walks of life.

Growing up in Westlawn was like being a member of the "Little Rascals", except a generation later. There were plenty of kids of all ages. My two main playmates were Kenneth Odom, a year younger, who lived next door; and Jimmy Eveland, two years younger, who lived just across the street. Jimmy's dad was an FBI agent. They had moved to Mobile from Minnesota. Behind their house was a work shed in which we were always building stuff--model boats, wooden guns, swords, slingshots, shields, bows, arrows, and blowguns--just to name a few items. I subscribed to "Boys Life" magazine, which was often the source of our ideas.

Not far away was our "playground" known as Wragg Swamp--a really wild swamp with wetlands and creeks in which there were fish, snakes, bullfrogs, and wild game of all sorts. The swamp was a main attraction to many kids in Westland, much to the horror of our parents. Not only could you get lost in there, but also there were oodles of poisonous cottonmouths and copperheads, and also areas of quicksand. We would actually jump into the quicksand bogs just for the fun of trying to get back out! If you couldn't do it, someone had to pull you out with a limb. On several occasions, we built some homemade watercraft to float down the creeks. The water was clean and relatively clear, a foot or two deep, but with a clean sandy bottom. We built a round boat, covered underneath with canvas called a "coracle" from "Boys Life". This boat carried two of us about 30 feet downstream before sinking. Another style of boat was based on the comic book "Pogo Possum"--picture the boat Albert and Pogo used. It was a rectangular wooden skiff, with two seats, and it actually floated--with us in it!

Of course our playground, Wragg Swamp, was lost during the late '50s when it was filled in for the construction of the malls--Springdale Plaza and Belle Aire--and the construction of the I-10 Interstate.

Besides my two buddies mentioned and me, other local kids in the "Rhea Street Gang" were the Sokols: Johnny and Kenny; the Chaffins: Gail, Lee, Sue, and Wayne; the Evelands: Johnny, Cathy, and Mary; the Biggers girls: Ann, Kay, and Donna; Jackie Lamb; and Wayne Mooney. After the Chaffins moved away, the Terrys moved in: Donna, Kay and their older brother.

Chapter 1

RHEA STREET GANG

Part 2

And there were battles. We had dirt clod fights, rubber gun shoot outs, bow and arrow battles with rubber stoppers, sword fights with swords made from coat hangers, acts of getting shot and falling 'in slow motion', wrestling, boxing, and bicycle and foot races. Most of us were very physical but were not into organized sports such as Little League or Park Football. We would rather dig a deep pit somewhere, camouflage it with sticks and leaves, and then try to get somebody (usually my sister) to fall in it. Great fun!

We built a four-story clubhouse and dared each other to jump off the top. We also made parachutes and would jump off Odom's garage.

As we got a little older, Kenneth, Jimmy, and I were allowed to ride the city bus into downtown. Of course buses were strictly segregated in the '50s --whites in the front and blacks in the back. The bus driver would enforce this regulation. I remember black maids with sacks and bundles, who had worked hard all day, having to get up and move to the back of the bus in order to give us white kids their seat! We didn't think much of it at the time. Of course now, looking back, those actions were shameful and wrong.

Anyway, the first stop was Hobby Land on lower Dauphin, where we eyed the model airplanes, and then on to the Army/Navy store where we bought throwing knives, canteens with belts, packs and, of course, "leggin's". Jimmy always wanted to go into Bonner Novelty, looking for fake vomit. When we got back home, we dressed in our gear and headed to a vacant area we called "The Field". It was located between Emogene Street at the Twin Oaks and Potter Drive. There, we would practice throwing knives at a hollow magnolia tree. There was a large hole about 3 ft. up from the ground and sometimes our knives were lost in that hole. Today, I am wondering if that tree is still there? If it is, there are several rusty throwing knives inside its hollow trunk!

JCS

Chapter 2

WESTLAWN SCHOOL

Most kids that lived in Westlawn attended the following schools: Westlawn Elementary, Sidney Phillips Jr. High, and Murphy High. I was in the first grade at Westlawn Elementary the first year it started (1949). Everything was brand new. The principal was Mary Montgomery. Some of the teachers that I remember were Mrs. Valda Wright, Mrs. Bess Owens, Miss Collier, Miss Steele, and Mrs. Hager. Mrs. Watson, Mrs. Grafton, and Miss Pearson.

Westlawn was different from other grammar schools in that a new "progressive" way of teaching was to be administered. In spite of that, we somehow learned to read and write; however, the main goal of Mrs. Mary Montgomery was to put on an elaborate pageant at the end of the school year. They were performed every year for 7 years. I mean those things were BIG productions! They weren't some little play on a little stage. Creating the pageants was like making a movie! They were performed outdoors in the playground behind the school on several acres of space. Huge colorful sets were painted, constructed, and erected. My mother, Jane Shaw was the set director for 7 years. She designed, painted, and supervised a whole crew of parents. Other parents made costumes, did carpentry, electrical, lighting, and sound setup. All this started sometime in the early spring and went on until the end of the school year.

The pageant themes were based loosely on different children's stories and Mrs. Savory, one of the parents, wrote the general script. I was in 6 pageants--first through the 6th grade. Some of the themes were: Looking Through the Looking Glass, Hansel and Gretel, Jack and the Beanstalk, The Wizard of Oz, Little Black Sambo, Charlotte's Web, and Alice in Wonderland.

Try-outs for the main characters began in the early spring. I tried out for various characters but was never chosen until the 6th grade. I was Little Wilber the Pig and Melvin McElroy was Big Wilber, in Charlotte's Web. My sister, Suzanne, was chosen as a main character just about every year. Anyway, if you were lucky enough to be one of the "main" characters then school was virtually over for you once rehearsals began.

Mrs. Montgomery herself was the director and-- weather permitting--there was a rehearsal every day until the pageant was finally performed. Each grade had a part and costumes. There were costumed tin soldiers, elves, fairies, dancers, acrobats, rabbits, pigs, glowworms, and even pancakes!

Bleachers were set up for the audience and there was always quite a crowd. The performance was at night with lighting, a spot light, recorded music for each scene, and a sound system for the narration of the story by one of the students.

It's too bad that some of these pageants weren't filmed and recorded, because they were really well done by very talented individuals. The sets were beautifully made, the stories and scripts were well written, and the costumes were very original. I had heard that one year Life Magazine was to photograph it but I don't think they showed up.

Chapter 3

UNIONTOWN

Back in the late '40s and early '50s, I spent some memorable times with my grandmother in Uniontown, Alabama. I would usually stay at my paternal grandmother Shaw's house. I was very young, but I remember that each of the five bedrooms had a small fireplace that burned coal, except for my grandmother's room, which had a potbelly stove.

In the front bedroom, lived my aunt Lucretia and her husband. The middle bedroom was where my ailing great-grandmother Fox stayed, and then there were two bachelor uncles (Foxes) in their bedrooms. I always slept in my grandmother's room with her (I was probably 6 or 7).

There was one bathroom with a flush toilet, but all the bedrooms had chamber pots so you didn't have to walk through the house to the bathroom during the cold winter.

The kitchen was very interesting. I would go in there with my grandmother and watch her cook. She was a wonderful cook and she prepared all the meals without any assistance. The stove was a large wood-

burning stove, and the water heater drew its heat from that stove. The water heater hissed like a steam engine when it got
really hot.

The coal supply was kept outside in the backyard near a fig tree. Firewood and kindling were kept dry in the wood shed.

Old Jake, a black man, was my only playmate. He did yard work and odd jobs for the family and was also my "babysitter".

He was very good-natured and didn't mind playing games. He liked to show me his missing finger, which he said that he had cut off in order to avoid going to war!

My two uncles and my aunt and her husband owned a store downtown. The store was the largest store in town and was named for my aunt--the Lucretia Fox Department Store. They also owned a barbershop and a beauty parlor that they leased out.

My grandmother's house was located about 4 or 5 blocks from the store. My uncles would walk to work but my aunt and her husband would drive their 1948 Plymouth. My aunt drove because her husband was crippled. Sometimes I would ride with them down to the store. Before my aunt started up the engine, she always put on "driving gloves". No women back then drove cars without wearing gloves!

The store was divided into 2 departments. The largest section was clothing and apparel. That's where the women clerked. The smaller section catered to mostly black men, who bought things like combs, knives, straight razors, tooth powder, love potions (yes, love potions), dice, hair oils and hair straighteners! One table was nothing but Vaseline...huge jars of it!

I liked hanging around in there with my uncle Dick, who would let me pick out a treat every now and then. I usually got a pocketknife...sometimes a switchblade!

Chapter 4
CALIFORNIA TRIP

Camping with family in Arizona

During the summer of 1956, my family decided to take a vacation trip to San Diego, California, where my sister Suzanne and I were born, and where my maternal grandparents, Joe and Aileen Mobley, still lived.

My father had bought a brand new Chevrolet station wagon, and we decided to camp at least once along the highway if we found a suitable spot. Olivia, our beloved black maid, was also going with us to visit a nephew there. Olivia had worked for my family for many years and helped raise my sister and me. She was like family.

Along with our luggage, we loaded the car with a large tent, camp stove, sleeping bags, and air mattresses, a cooler, and some canned food.

The first night was spent in Longview, Texas, at the Dun Roamin' Motel along U.S. hwy. 80. We had stayed there on other trips out west, so we were familiar with the accommodations. We got two rooms--one for my family and one for Olivia. The proprietors had no problem renting a room to a black person. However, the further west we traveled, the more problems we had getting restaurants and motels to accept Olivia. In New Mexico and west Texas, she was only allowed to enter restaurants through the back door and was fed in the kitchen. Motels would not rent her a room, but said it was ok for her to sleep in our station wagon. Of course this was upsetting to Olivia and embarrassing to us, but that was the way it was back then.

On the third night we decided to camp out. As the sun was setting we found a perfect place to stop. By then, we were in the desolate Arizona desert and pulled off the road at an old windmill with a stock tank and a small grove of mesquite trees. We got the tent up, cranked up the stove, and heated a pot of canned beef stew. Our air mattresses were blown up and we settled in for the night. Olivia chose the car again.

Although it was summertime, the desert night was cold and our cheap sleeping bags were not much of a comfort. When the morning finally arrived, we were surprised that all four air mattresses were flat! Unfortunately, we had pitched the tent, which had a canvas floor, over several mesquite limbs. If you are familiar with mesquite, you know that they have long sharp thorns that can even penetrate a car tire. That's why we were on the cold ground by morning.

After breakfast Suzanne and I went over to the concrete watering trough to brush our teeth. The windmill was pumping a steady stream of fresh water, so we began brushing. Suddenly Suzanne took off running without saying a word. I heard a loud shhhhhh!...looked down and saw rattlesnakes (sidewinders) everywhere coming out from under the edge of the trough where we had been sticking our feet! There was a whole den of them, and needless to say, this got me running too.

Daddy had brought along a.22 rifle and he shot quite a few of them. We cut off some of the small rattles for souvenirs.

As we drove along, Olivia, who had never been in the west, kept commenting about the treeless, hot Arizona desert..."Lord have mercy! They ought to give this place back to the Indians!"

Seeing a roadside curio stand with a lot of painted pottery, my mother wanted to stop and buy something. A heavyset Indian woman was sitting in the shade of a large umbrella. My father said, "Let me handle this. I know how to bargain with these people."

We sat in the car as he walked over to her.

"Qué cuanto...ah...qué mucho de pots?" stammered my father.

The woman just looked at him and finally said in perfect English, "Do you want to know the price of my pottery? Well, they are different prices!" Daddy bought the cheapest one on the shelf.

California was a welcomed relief from the hot trip and we had a good time visiting with my grandparents. They stayed at home while my family and Olivia went to Disneyland, which had just opened. We also went to Knott's Berry Farm and La Jolla along the coast. One day my grandfather, father, and myself went deep-sea fishing in Mexican waters. We caught sea bass, barracuda, bonita, and yellowtail tuna. We used anchovies for bait and sea lions were robbing our bait. I was shocked when the captain shot several of the sea lions with a shotgun. They weren't killed...just scared them away.

One of the reasons we had gone to California was because my father, who was a cartoonist, had an interview with Walt Disney Studios. Before the war he had drawn some of the Alley Oop comic strip for V.T. Hamlin, and also had drawn a comic strip for the Navy during war times.

He was not hired although they were very impressed with his work. At the time Disney was not hiring cartoonists. They were sinking their money into the expansion of Disneyland.
Epilog:
Olivia Clark worked for us for many more years

and finally retired to her original hometown of Meridian, Mississippi. She stayed in touch with my family for many years after that and died at the age of 100!

Chapter 5

Parental Conspiracy

There I was...standing against the wall, inside the Sidney Phillips Jr. High gymnasium, nervously trying to look like I was having a good time!

It was a Friday night "sock hop", and my parents had insisted that I go. Much to my reluctance, I donned the customary black pants, pink shirt, clip-on skinny black tie, white socks, white buck shoes, and light blue sport coat...ready for the dance!

"Now, we'll drop you off at eight and pick you up at ten", said my mother.

Great! Two hours of extreme torture! To me it was going to seem like two days!

I had arrived at the gym, and immediately looked for a dark corner, but the gym was brilliantly lit up. I found a curtain against the wall near the refreshment stand, so I decided to try to "blend" into the curtain while sipping on a coke.

The music was supplied by a record player which was piped through the intercom system...turned up to full volume. Kids with dates were all over the dance floor doing extremely complicated looking dance steps in their sock feet. The songs were familiar..."Young Love", "April Love", "Tootie Fruitie", "Tammy", "Blue Velvet", "Boney Maroney", and "Great Balls of Fire"--just to mention a few.

One of my 8th grade classmates strolled by and happened to recognize me. It was Clarence Springer... with a date! Even if it was Wanda Wilson, it was still a date. Maybe I had a chance after all!

"You want to dance with my date?" he asked. "She'll dance with anybody!"

"Well, I dunno, Clarence...I'm sorta drinkin' this Coke right now."

"Aw, go ahead--she 'bout wore me out!"

"Well, OK but let's wait for a slow one."

Wanda was several inches taller and probably outweighed me by at least 25 pounds, but we "shuffled" around on the dance floor to a Pat Boone song. When the next song was a fast rock and roller, I told her, "I don't know how to 'bop'", and started back toward the refreshment stand.

But before I could make my getaway, Wanda gabbed my arm like a vise, swung me around, and said, "OOH! Chuck Berry!"
So away we went. Wanda took the lead, and I tried to follow. I'm sure we were quite a sight!

Well, the last hour dragged on, but finally came to

an end. I went outside looking for my ride, thinking I'll never have to go through that again!

When I got in the car, my mother asked how I enjoyed it? "Oh, it was great...I had a great time", I lied.

"Good, because we are enrolling you in a ballroom dance class!"

It was the horror of horrors! A conspiracy cooked up by one of the mothers at a garden club meeting. So, the idea spread throughout our neighborhood, as each parent thought it was time their sons learned a few "social graces". At least I would have company. Several of my buddies on my street were to suffer the same fate.

The lessons were given on Monday nights at a private dance studio on Dauphin Street. I think it was a ballet school during the day. Needless to say, Mondays in my neighborhood were especially dreaded, not just because we had school, but we knew what was coming up that night!

There were lots of girls in the class, and we were "matched up" at random. After a few lessons, we tried to choose our place in line carefully so we would match up with one of the better-looking girls.

The dances we were forced to learn were not exactly current. In fact they were about a generation off. We learned the foxtrot, cha-cha, waltz, jitterbug, and yes, the polka!

As the weeks dragged on, however, I actually started to enjoy the classes--even looked forward to them!

When I finally graduated from dance school and wound up at another sock hop, I never did get a chance to polka!

Chapter 6

MY FIRST CAR

Author (left) with Ken Odom and '49 Willys Jeepster.

My first car was a 1949 Willys Jeepster convertible. My parents paid $395 for it in 1959 when I turned 16. It had a 4 cylinder flathead engine. Although it was not 4 wheel drive, my friends and I would drive on the sand at Gulf Shores and camp on the beach. If the car got stuck, we would let some air out of the tires and drive on. It was so light that it would go right over the sand dunes.

I had a lot of fun in that car, but it was a "rolling death trap". The floorboard was rusted out so you could see the pavement below. The doors would not latch and would swing open on a turn. Nothing worked on the instrument panel, and if it rained, you would get wet even though the top was up! When the battery went dead, I had to park on a hill and pop the clutch to get it started. During the summer of 1962, I delivered eggs all over the city of Mobile and paid more for tires and parts than what little I earned on the egg route. A few years later I sold the Jeepster to a neighbor for $100. A week later she returned the car and wanted her money back!

Chapter 7

MURPHY BAND

When I was old enough for high school in 1958, there was only one public high school for white kids in Mobile, and that was Murphy High. So the student body was overflowing. It was like a college with thousands of students. When my class graduated in 1961, it was the largest class of graduating seniors in Murphy's history, before or since--1050 students. The principal during my years was a man named Hodges.

In junior high, I had been in the band as a trumpet player for three years, and went on to join the high school band at Murphy. The band director was Ira Swingle, who was a virtuoso musician, and could play several instruments, mostly the piano and trumpet. He had "perfect pitch", which meant he could hear a car horn out on the street and tell you, "That was a C sharp!"

Other subjects were Latin, math, physics, biology, history, civics, and English. I made average grades. Band took up much of my time, especially during football season, which meant long hours of practice after school for the half-time shows. Swingle was short tempered and screamed at us on the practice field.

During Mardi Gras, marching in parades was always hazardous. Civil unrest between Blacks and Whites was at a peak at this time, and most of the bands had to have protection from the National Guard who marched along with us. Swingle put the larger band members to the outside (I was on the inside), and before a parade, they prepared for "battle". Trombone players taped knife blades to the end of their slides, the drummers carried blackjacks, and many members carried clubs.

Night parades were the most dangerous, especially in areas like lower Dauphin St. and Broad, where there would be a sudden ambush! Young black men would rush in and briefly start a ruckus. A few tried to hit the end of our instruments, giving the player, a bloody lip. We were also spat on, and had objects thrown at us.

But band members fought back, especially the drummers, who would whack people with their drumsticks if they got too close. I remember the bass drummer hitting his drum on the downbeat and the crowd on the upbeat! On one occasion, someone jumped up behind the tuba player, grabbed the top rim of the horn, and slammed it and the player backwards to the pavement--hard! This prompted the tuba player to pull out the heavy brass mouthpiece and bludgeon the attacker over the head. More attackers came then, kicking and shoving us. I got kicked in the shin. A girl clarinet player was hurt when her instrument was hit, injuring her throat. Swingle was hollering for us to just run forward until we were past the danger zone--which we did.

After that incident, the number of National Guard

soldiers was increased and the violence decreased. The more parades we marched in, the more the school was paid, so I think we marched in every single Mardi Gras parade, rain or shine! I have hated Mardi Gras ever since!

Chapter 8

DIXIE DIVISION BAND

Part 1

One day a National Guard sergeant came up to the band room and asked for volunteers to temporarily join the Dixie Division Band for a 4-day trip to Miami, Florida for the purpose of marching in a Veterans parade. Mr. Swingle said that the school would not grant an excuse for missing classes on those days, but if we wanted to go, he wouldn't stop us. I immediately volunteered along with fellow trumpeter Gene Chapman. There may have been a few others (?). With a letter of parental permission, we were actually sworn in to the National Guard at Ft. Whiting Armory, issued military uniforms, and were told we would be released from service after the trip. In addition to the fatigues, we were issued Confederate uniforms, which were the dress of the Dixie Division Band. And we were to be paid for our service!

C-119 Flying Boxcars were built for transporting cargo--not human beings--but that's what we were to fly on to Miami.

On a sunny morning, we boarded the plane at Bates Field in Mobile. It would be my first flight on an airplane. There were no seats inside the cavernous cargo plane, just a fold down canvas bench, running along both sides of the fuselage, and it was mandatory to wear a parachute for duration of the flight.

Parachute briefing by sergeant: "Now men, I'm gonna show you this one, and only one, time how to put on your parachute. These straps that go between your legs have to be like so...if not, when you pull your ripcord, you will lose your 'family jewels'... if you know what I mean! So pay close attention. Also, if you see that red light over the emergency exit go on while we're in the air, the door will be blown, and you will exit the airplane. And if you don't jump, you will be pushed out!"

Now that we were all scared stiff, the engines were revved, and we took off. As the plane banked and gained altitude, we remained on our bench seats. C-119's were not pressurized and the noise was almost unbearable. Talking was not an option, unless you could read lips. When we reached our cruising altitude of only 5000 ft., the horror of horrors--the red light began flashing! I was to be the second one in line to jump. Just then, the sergeant came out of the cockpit, waving his arms, shaking his head, and pointing at the light.

It went off and we realized it must have been some sort of malfunction. Whew!

Chapter 8

DIXIE DIVISION BAND

Part 2

The cargo bay of the plane had no windows, except for a small portal in the emergency exit door. There were about 50 or so people on board, and we took turns looking out. The "restroom" was a funnel attached to a hose that went through a hole in the floor.

We landed that evening in Miami. Then we were given a "hygiene talk" by the Sergeant, before boarding a bus for Miami Beach. We stayed in several small hotels on Flagler Avenue. Chapman and I shared a room. After band practice the next day, we went to the Fontaine Belau Hotel where we played for the vets and some politicians. We all shook hands with Governor Patterson of Alabama, and then had a huge buffet dinner.

The next day's American Legion Parade, in which we marched, was uneventful and long. We took off later that night, headed for Mobile. On the night flight, we were allowed, one at a time, to ride in the cockpit, which was a real treat. We flew all night, landing back at Bates Field early the next morning.

Back at school, I learned that I was in big trouble. I was told to report immediately to Dean Moore's office. We were all facing suspension from school for cutting classes.

However, we got off with a mere admonishment by the Dean...so I thought. Each of my teachers knew what we had done, and in my case, I was called to the front, in each of my classes, and told to give a public apology to the class. Miss Hope and Mrs. Reynolds said they were appalled at my behavior! Ouch!

JCS

Chapter 9

BIRMINGHAM PARADE

The first trip with the Dixie Division Band nearly got me suspended from school; nevertheless, I made one more trip with them. But this time it was on a weekend, so I would not have to miss any classes. Again, the band needed additional musicians for another veterans' parade--this time in Birmingham. It was a repeat of mostly the same group of Murphy Band members that went on the first trip, so we knew what to expect. Instead of Bates Field, however, we were to fly from Brookley AFB in a C-119 Flying Boxcar, and return that evening.

On an early Saturday morning, we boarded the plane, put on our parachutes, and sat in the cargo bay, awaiting takeoff. Out on the runway, we proceeded to take off, but about half way down the runway, we heard a loud explosion, and the plane slowed to a stop. We had blown a tire. Another C-119 was brought out, and we unloaded instruments and equipment, and boarded the new plane. Unbelievably, the same thing happened again! A blown tire just before takeoff! A third plane (C-119) was rolled out and we got on it.

The pilot came into the cargo bay and said, "You guys better make sure you got your parachutes on, 'cause this time we're goin' up...no matter what! This is the last bird we've got!"

With that said, the pilot revved up the engines to an extremely high (and loud!) pitch...released the brakes...and we climbed into the clear morning sky, headed for Birmingham.

The rest of the trip was uneventful, except for a chance meeting of my friend Gene Chapman's brother in law. After the parade, Gene and I were walking along a sidewalk when someone sitting on a bench called Gene's name. It was Emmet Philyaw, who was married to Gene's older sister, Vivian. At the time, Emmet was in the National Guard, but not connected to our unit. He was dressed in uniform, with rifle and gear, and happened to be on assignment in Birmingham (he lived in Mobile). We stopped and talked for a while until our bus came.

Years later, Emmet Philyaw became a laymen preacher, witnessing to inmates in jails and prisons all over the state. He founded "Wings of Life", which is a mission and shelter for the homeless in downtown Mobile.

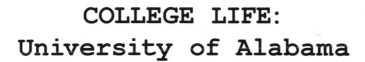

COLLEGE LIFE:
University of Alabama

Chapter 10

First Semester, 1961

During my first year of college at the University of Alabama, I lived in a campus dormitory--Summerville Hall. My roommate was Jim Burns who was a senior, scheduled to graduate with a BA in education at the end of the fall semester. He was the son of Cranford Burns, who was the Superintendent of Schools in Mobile County at that time.

Jim was a dorm counselor and was entitled to a private room. However, due to a large student population that year, he was forced to share his small room--with me. He was not exactly thrilled with that and hoped that I could soon be transferred to someone else's room.

Needless to say, we were cramped. But Jim Burns was a very friendly, outgoing, and polite person, and we soon got along just fine. He helped me adjust to college life and introduced me to his friends, most of whom were seniors also. Jim was political. He was running for president of the student council but was defeated by Ted Seay. Ironically, after Jim graduated, Ted Seay wound up as my roommate during my second semester--in Jim's old room! Of course Ted wanted me out too but that's another story.

But getting back to Jim's friends, I remember the ones in the dorm were somewhat eccentric. There was Big Fred, who never bathed. He was a biology major and liked to argue about religion..."Man, when you die, you die and that's it!" Burns was more open-minded and took both sides. Being a Southern Baptist, I held to my "fundamentalist" beliefs.

There was George Dolan, a law student with a very dry wit, Catholic, and loved to have a steak and a beer at The Chuckor restaurant in downtown Tuscaloosa. In the room next to ours were Pat Ballard and George Saklaredes (Greek), both chemical engineer majors from Birmingham. Across the hall was Billy Williams, who like me, was a freshman from Mobile.

For transportation, I had brought a bicycle, borrowed from Vince O'Connor. Jim had a Volkswagen beetle, as did just about every student who was lucky enough to own a car.

Studying in the dorm was virtually impossible. Someone was always dropping by, usually Jim's beatnik buddies. They would put on a Dave Brubeck record and start smoking. The whole dorm was full of tobacco smoke. I didn't smoke but probably inhaled enough smoke to be a smoker! There were many heated and sometimes philosophical discussions going on about every topic imaginable. Most of my studying, what little I did, was done in the library with Williams, who was a disturbance himself.

Summerville Hall had a basement with a TV and vending machines. I remember hearing someone say, "Hey, let's go downstairs and watch the Bear."

"What?? A bear...what bear?" I was so dumb and naive, I didn't know who Bear Bryant was! I thought we were maybe going down to watch "Gentle Ben"!

Occasionally, there were "dorm swaps". That was when a few brave coeds from a girls' dorm (miles away) were allowed to visit a men's' dorm after dark in order to "socialize" in the basement. Typically, the girls that showed up were what you might call "desperate"! Music was played, maybe one couple would dance, but the rest of us just sat around in the dark.

ROTC was a required course then, and you had a choice of Army or Air Force. I chose Army. My company commander was the aforementioned Ted Seay, who was also the president of the student council. ROTC drill was held once a week (weather permitting), during which there was a lot of marching around on the Quadrangle. On Governor's Day, George Wallace would show up for "Pass and Review". He would stand and salute until we all passed by.

After a few months, I became one of the buglers (there were 4 of us), so all we had to do was play Assembly at the beginning of drill and Taps at the end. We buglers were not required to march, so we sat around under the oaks while the rest of them drilled away.

Summerville Hall was not far from the Black Warrior River, which was nothing but a toxic sewer at that time. The water had an acrid, chemical stench and, released vapors of volatile gas! Also, at night the air was so polluted, it was literally hard to breath outside. All this pollution was from the Gulf States Paper Mill, which thankfully, was shut down in the '80s.

Directly behind the dorm was a pond. I don't know the purpose of it, but it was full of frogs and snakes. One cold night as Several of us were sitting around the dorm, I don't remember how it came up, but someone dared me to swim across the pond. I accepted the dare and everyone went outside that night to watch me drown! Wearing just a pair of jeans, I slipped into the cold water, trying to catch my breath. I had no idea how deep it was but it was over my head. I swam as fast as I could to the other side, hoping that all the resident snakes were well into hibernation. When I reached the other side, I ran back around to the dorm where the onlookers pronounced me insane--but I won the bet!

Epilog: Several years ago (I don't remember the year), I read in the Mobile Press-Register that Jim Burns had been murdered. I don't remember the details, except that it happened one night, when someone broke into his family home and Jim was killed.

Chapter 11

SECOND SEMESTER, 1962

"Roomie, shut up that racket! I'm trying to get some sleep!" said my roommate, Jim Burns, as I was nervously playing drum cadences on my math book with two pencils. It was final exam time, Jan. 1962, at the University of Alabama, and I was high on a drug many college students were taking back then-- amphetamine or "speed". I didn't know it was dope. It was just this little capsule that you paid 50 cents for, and it kept you awake all night so you could study. But I guess it helped, because I aced the math exam, which brought my grade up from a "D" to a "C".

Well, old Jim graduated and married his long time girl friend from Judson College and they both became schoolteachers. So at the beginning of my second semester as a geology major, I was still in the dorm counselor's room, enjoying more space, until the new counselor showed up. It was my old ROTC company commander and class president, Ted Seay. He remembered me from ROTC and said that my stay in 'his' room was temporary; since, as a dorm counselor, he was entitled to a private room. Ted, like Jim, was very friendly, outgoing, and, unlike Jim-- very religious. He was from Enterprise, Alabama.

The second thing Ted said to me was "Are you going to the ROTC Ball?" I said no, that I hadn't planned on it. He said "well, you're goin' as a blind date with my date's roommate." So the next week end, we were headed to Montevallo College in Ted's Vauxhall (car) to pick up our dates. It so happened that my blind date was a very pretty blond named Elizabeth Glasgow. Both girls were so excited just to be getting away from Montevallo. None other than the Tommy Dorsey Band held the ball in the Foster Auditorium with live music. It was formal and we had to wear our ROTC uniforms. Ted even had a sword since he was an officer. We had a nice time. I actually danced with my date a few times. We took them back to their college the next day.

After a few weeks, I was relocated to a new dorm room with Billy, my old classmate from Mobile. He was a pre-law major and had two older brothers attending the university. Together, Billy and I bought an old wrecked Cushman motor scooter. The front fork and tire were bent at a 45-degree angle, and when riding it, you had to lean out on the opposite side in order to attain balance--not the safest form of transportation!! But we rode all over campus on that scooter, both of us leaning out on the starboard side!

Like his brothers, Billy was tall and lanky, about 6' 2", so we were like Mutt and Jeff. He had a good sense of humor and we got along pretty well, but toward the end of the semester, we began to get on each other's nerves. One day we got into a short fight in our room. I forget just what it was about, but I remember really losing my temper, which I rarely do. I cursed him and then grabbed him by the shoulders and slung him against a mirror so hard that it cracked. His arm was bleeding slightly where I had grabbed him. "Look what you did to me!" he said, looking at his arms. As the adrenalin subsided in me, I didn't know whether he would retaliate or not. He probably could have laid me low, but I think he was so shocked by my sudden "attack." Anyway, I don't remember whether either of us apologized or not, but after that, we became good friends again for the rest of the semester.

Chapter 12

SOPHOMORE YEAR, 1962-3

As a sophomore at the University of Alabama--1962, I moved away from Summerville Hall and into off campus housing. I teamed up with my old buddies from Mobile, Ronnie Stevens and Kenneth Odom. I had known Odom ever since I was about seven years old, when his family was my family's next-door neighbor. Stevens, I had known from the Murphy High Band. We were both trumpet players.

At the beginning of the Fall semester, we moved into a large, two story house. Our landlady was a Miss Adams. She lived downstairs and we renters lived upstairs. Odom and Stevens were roommates and I was in another room with a student from Winston County--I don't remember his name. One other student lived out back in a garage apartment.

We were doing well. I was a geology major taking my first actual course in geology. Odom was an accounting major and Stevens, physics. We had brought a set of weights and dumb bells from home, and each of us exercised for a few minutes in the afternoon after class.

A few days later we started getting little "complaint" notes from the landlady. She wrote that we made too much noise walking around. She wrote down how we should walk: "Come down on the heels of your feet and roll onto the ball portion..."
So, we tried to learn the "Adams walk". The next complaint note was about the noise we made when lifting weights--"you boys are making too much noise with your toys up there". We tried to be quieter.

Then came the "chores"! She had us paint her entire porch, feed her cat, spruce up her house, do this, stop doing that! This went on for weeks until we decided to move out and find another apartment. But when we told her we were leaving, she got very angry and said that we could do no such thing. We had signed a six-month lease and she was going to hold us to it.

At about this time we learned that the student living in the garage apartment was planning to move. He told us that after Miss Adams learned of his "disloyalty", she came to his door that night and tried to get inside his room. But the room was locked and when he peered out, he could see that she had a butcher knife in her hand! The next morning, as this student was trying to leave, Miss Adams hit him with a shovel, injuring his arm and shoulder. Well, after we learned of this episode, we were dead set on getting out of there--lease or no lease!

Shortly afterward, Miss Adams left town. She told us that she was going on a vacation to Florida, and that we were to feed her cat while she was away. The day after she left, we decided that we were going to find our lease papers that we had signed. We knew they must be in her house somewhere. That night, after feeding the cat, we sneaked inside her downstairs living area, found her desk, and started looking through her stuff. Sure enough, we found all three of our leases and tore them out of her lease book. We took the papers back upstairs, put them in a metal tray, and lit a match, leaving no evidence!

While she was still away, we found another apartment on 6th Street, several blocks away, and moved in. It was a four-room, downstairs apartment so each of us (Odom, Stevens, I) had a private room. The fourth room was a kitchen.

We reported Miss Adams to the Dean of Student Housing, and we found out that she had a long record of complaints going back several years from many other students and that she had once been a mental patient in Bryce Institute! She was a "psycho"...with a butcher knife!

John Craig Shaw

Chapter 13

THE CORSAIRS

When I was in the band at the University of Alabama, I was also in a dance orchestra called "The Corsairs". The year was 1965. One job was to play for the Monroeville High School prom that spring. We travelled to Monroeville Country Club from Tuscaloosa after class. We were in 2 cars and arrived that evening and got set up.

We had "hand-me-down" sheet music from a band member's father's music store, and most of the tunes were Glenn Miller tunes and older. Some of the kids got up and danced but most were wondering when we were going to play some "real" music! None of them knew how to jitterbug. This was music for their parents!

One "new" song we had was "Autumn Leaves" (Wow--now you're goovin'!) in which I played a solo part--but I think I messed it up!

I don't remember how much we were paid, but it wasn't much. One of our cars, a Studebaker Hawke (you don't see them around anymore), broke down on the way back to Tuscaloosa. We spent all of our pay, plus some of our own money, to have the car repaired, and got back about sunrise!

The short-lived Corsairs bit the dust soon after that road trip! If we could have turned the clock back about 20 years, we might have been a success. Today, Big Band music has made a big comeback and is popular with all ages.

Chapter 14

SPELUNKERS

Part 1

While in college at the University of Alabama, I joined a Spelunking Club. This club was composed of young folks of 'no fear' and not much sense, who loved nothing better than to crawl around in wet, dark, muddy, bat infested, holes in the ground, called caves. I was hooked from the start, visiting my first 'wild' cave with a National Speleological Society group from Birmingham. The cave was Guffy Cave and after that trip, I joined the university chapter.

On just about every free week end afterwards, I found myself, along with my friends, Gene Chapman, Craig Weaver, John Hauer, Bob Gamble, and a 'wildman' named Hooper plus his girl friend, piling into Weaver's VW Beetle and Hauer's Buick, 'Big Bertha', for two days and a night of spelunking.

North Alabama is graciously endowed with limestone, and thus, has many caves, as well as some beautiful commercial caves such as Cathedral Caverns near

Huntsville. But we wanted the real thing--'wild caves'! These were caves that you entered at your own risk. We wore hardhats with mounted carbide lanterns which were heavy because they were filled with water, so the first thing you did when you entered a cave was to pick up a handful of clay and stick it to the back of your hardhat as a counter weight. We carried cable ladders, candles, matches, water, snacks, and extra carbide...and sometimes string to mark our route through complicated passageways.

One of our favorite caves to explore was Taluca Cave in Morgan County, near the Tennessee River. It was an extensive cave with all the ingredients of interest: nice formations, large rooms, a 'maze', plenty of bats, underground streams and pools, and long claustrophobic crawl spaces which were extremely tight, muddy and slick. One crawl space was called 'The Noodle' because it was just that--it was so tight, you had to put your arms forward and 'worm' your way through. As skinny as I was, I had trouble getting through. Another tight spot was called 'The Pop Up'. This required taking off your helmet, turning your head sideways while exhaling and pushing yourself through a vertical shaft no bigger than a chimney! Spelunking is definitely not for fat people.

Besides getting lost (or stuck in one of the tight spots), there was a real danger of the main entrance becoming flooded during heavy rains, and thereby temporarily becoming trapped inside.

We would leave after classes on Friday and arrive after dark at the mouth of the cave where we set up camp for the night. Hooper always brought along a large jug of his home brew that he made at his apartment. He cooled it in a spring, which flowed into the cave. Hooper was our leader. He was from Huntsville and knew the cave better than anyone else.

The entrance was wide but low, and after a short distance, you would be in a room that was lit by daylight! A sizable hole had been blasted out of the roof by Confederate troops during the Civil War in order to mine a huge pile of bat guano (sodium nitrate), which was used in the making of gunpowder. The guano was still there, piled up about 6 ft. high.

Chapter 14

SPELUNKERS

Part 2

Taluca cave was easy to get lost in because of so many similar passageways. When entering 'the maze', there was only one way in and out...the rest of the passageways were all dead ends.

On one trip, Hooper could not go but several of us decided we were familiar enough with the cave to go without him. When we got to the entrance, we had forgotten the string, so we decided to use wooden matches to mark our way through the maze. We stuck a match in the soft clay every 5 or 10 feet until we got into the main tunnel known as 'Lincoln Tunnel'. We explored the cave for several hours.

After visiting the 'Big Room' at the back of the cave, we began heading back out. Everything went well until we got to the maze area. We could not find our 'match trail'! We crawled around through passage after passage until we were totally exhausted, but could not find a single match. And to make things worse, our carbide was running low.

To conserve our carbide and our energy, we decided to use just one light, and we plopped down on the cave floor to rest. We thought about rescue. Would anyone come after us if we didn't show up by Monday? Putting the thought from our heads, we decided to give the maze another try, but it was just more dead ends.

At one point in the maze, there was a sloping tunnel that we had already been through countless times. I was so weary and so covered from head to toe with wet mud that I just dropped and slid down the slippery slope. When I got to the bottom, I looked down, and there was a single match, barely visible because it had been smashed down into the soft clay. I hollered for the others and we began looking for more matches. Looking down one of the many tunnels, sure enough, were the standing matches-- and our way back out!

But more bad luck. It had rained while we were in the cave, and the small stream at the entrance was rapidly rising. We knew we had no time to lose. Entering the stream, we inched along on our backs with just inches of breathing room until we were finally out of Taluca Cave. Cold, wet, and totally exhausted, I was never so glad to be breathing the warm muggy air of the outside again! JCS

Chapter 15

Summer of '64

During the hot month of July 1964, Congress passed the Civil Rights Act, and President Johnson signed it into law. I was taking Organic Chemistry that summer at the University of Alabama. George Wallace had stood in the door the previous Summer, trying unsuccessfully, to block the first Black students, Vivian Malone and James Hood, from attending the all white university.

That Summer was a hotbed of civil unrest, especially at the University of Alabama, which is in the city of Tuscaloosa, where many K.K.K. members lived, including the Imperial Wizard Bobby Shelton.

At the time, I think most of the student body was against integration. In fact, I didn't know a single soul who was for it, although I'm sure there were some. I was in the Million Dollar Band, and it was feared that the band might become integrated. And probably, there was the same feeling about the football team. Today, that sort of thinking would probably be called "racism", and rightly so. I don't think Whites hated Blacks-- although some undoubtedly did-- we just grew up separately and didn't know many Black people, other than our family maids.

Of course we were wrong back then about the separation of the two races. Black people should have the same rights, freedoms, and opportunities as anyone else, and change was long overdue.

I was living in an off-campus apartment with my friends, Gene Chapman, Ronnie Stevens, and Ken Odom. We tried to stay out of trouble, but we were curious to see history in the making. Many civil rights sympathizers began coming down from northern states, and there was a general feeling of resentment among locals. There was rioting downtown, "sit ins", and some campus violence. Morrison's' Cafeteria was at the end of our block, and I remember a "sit in" by a group of young Black people. We watched as the Tuscaloosa PD and the Klan went inside, grabbed the participants who were eating lunch, and literally threw them out of the restaurant.

One evening as some friends and I were going to a movie downtown, we noticed people just standing around outside. No one was going in. I went up to the window to buy a ticket and was tapped on the shoulder by a middle-aged man. When I turned around, he said, "I don't think you want to go in there!" When I said that I did, he said, "I don't think you understand. There's N----rs in there!... and you do not want to go in there!" He was very forceful that time and I realized he was probably a Klan member. So I didn't go in, nor did anyone else as far as I know.

Another time the movie star Jack Palance came to Tuscaloosa, and we went downtown to see him. There was a misunderstanding as to why he was in town.

Blacks thought he was there to support the civil rights movement, but I don't think that was the case. Anyway, while he was at a local movie theater, a race riot broke out, and there was a fire in the theater. The fire and the riot were extinguished, but afterwards, the whole campus was put on an 8 pm curfew.

Some weeks later, after the curfew was lifted, it was announced that the K.K.K. was going to have an open meeting at a ball diamond north of town. Out of curiosity, some of my friends wanted to go, and I joined them. That night the ball field was filled with spectators. Klan meetings were usually secret and I think most people just wanted to see what went on at such an event.

The field was all lit up and there was a podium about where the pitcher's mound was. The Klan members were all dressed in white robes but their faces were not covered. There were even some children dressed in robes. Soon, a speaker came to the podium and introduced the Imperial Wizard, Bobby Shelton. The essence of his speech was, "Let's not start any trouble, but if they start it, we will damn sure finish it! We will fight 'em with sticks, bricks, baseball bats, axe handles, or whatever it takes to drive these agitators back where they came from!"

A huge cross behind the podium was then lit, and the whole night sky was aglow. People were cheering and stomping their feet in the bleachers. Shelton went on with his speech, but then real violence broke out. Shots started coming from the darkness beyond the outfield and toward the crowd! Some of the bullets were hitting the cross, and everyone in the bleachers, including us, got down underneath.

Bobby Shelton remained defiant, a prime target, but kept on with his speech! "Don't let a few shots bother you. Stand up to 'em!" he shouted over the loud speaker. Then, many of the robed Klan members began running toward the sound of the shooting. We were running for the car!

Afterwards, I think we were ashamed to have attended such an event. I certainly had no liking for the K.K.K.! But, as foolish college kids, we were out for a lark and something different. Our curiosity could have gotten us shot!

It was a long hot summer, but I got through Organic Chemistry with an A and a B.

Chapter 16
MILLION DOLLAR BAND

Author (right) with Ron Stevens

I knew Ronnie Stevens when I was in the Murphy High School band. We were both trumpet players, but he was far better than I was. When he came to the University of Alabama in 1962, he talked me into joining the Million Dollar band. The band director, Col. Carlton Butler, said he needed more trumpets, and allowed us to tryout. Anyway, our auditions were ok and we joined the band at mid semester as alternates. For some reason Col. Butler got Ronnie and me mixed up. He called me 'Stevens' and Ronnie, 'Shaw'. We were in the band for 2 years, and he never did get our names straightened out! On the practice field, Col Butler could holler louder than cannon fire! So when he bellowed, "STEVENS!! GET IN LINE!!" I knew he meant me, not Stevens.

As one of the top teams in the nation, Alabama wound up playing Oklahoma in the Orange Bowl. The band did a pre-game show and a half time show. President Kennedy was there, and he sat on one team's side the first half, and then switched sides for the second. During the pre-game show, there was a band dressed as Revolutionary War soldiers with a color guard. The color guard had rifles, and after we played the National Anthem, the rifles were fired, making a tremendous boom. I don't think the Secret Service knew that was going to happen, because they suddenly stood up and huddled around the President. Someone said that they had their guns drawn.

Fast forward to November 1963--I was still in the band. We were on the practice field just before lunch. One of the trumpet players came running on to the field, saying something about President Kennedy. "Kennedy's been shot!" he said. "Yeah, sure"...we heard what he said, but no one believed him, because he was always pulling pranks. It was not until I got back to my apartment, that I found out that he was telling the truth. Everyone was crowded around radios, as we listened to Walter Cronkite give the grim news of JFK's assassination.

Classes were cancelled for the rest of the week due to the assassination, and also because of Thanksgiving. My sister, Suzanne and myself, left Tuscaloosa to join family members in Uniontown, Alabama. When we arrived, we learned that many of the White townsfolk were not sad at all about the assassination--in fact, we heard of jubilant parties to celebrate it!

After the Iron Bowl (Alabama vs Auburn), Alabama was due to play in the Sugar Bowl in New Orleans. On the train from Mobile to New Orleans, I noticed a lot more sand dunes along the coast...but it wasn't sand, it was snow. The Gulf coast had a rare snowfall and it was headed for New Orleans. People were so excited because many had never seen snow. Before the band could do the pre-game show, or Alabama could play Ole Miss, the field had to be cleared of several inches of snow. Yes, we won the game, and the band (still in our uniforms) joined thousands of drunken Alabama fans...all headed for one destination...Pat O'Brien's.

During my junior year, I dropped out of the band, and got more serious with my major and minor subjects: Geology and Chemistry. I made A's and B's in Geology with average grades in mostly everything else, except Calculus, which I flunked twice. I graduated from the University in January 1966 with a C+ average.

Not anxious to drop my college deferment, I applied and was accepted to graduate school at the University of Hawaii in the Dept. of Oceanography. A new adventure was ahead!

GRADUATE SCHOOL:
UNIVERSITY OF HAWAII

Chapter 17

FIRST SEMESTER, 1966

Part 1

When I first arrived in Honolulu, I was plastered! It was in Jan. 1966 and I was on my way to the University of Hawaii to begin my first semester of graduate school in the study of oceanography. The flight happened to be a "champagne flight", and the stewardesses kept pouring all the way from L.A. to Honolulu! I didn't know a soul in Hawaii, but I did meet a nice family on the plane who took me with them to their hotel in Waikiki. The cost of my room was ten dollars a night, which I thought was outrageous.

Classes didn't start for another few weeks, and I stayed on at the hotel while looking for a place to live. The dorms were full. After looking for about two weeks, I found nothing I could afford and finally decided to forget grad school and go back to Alabama.

I met two other students, Dick Conner and Steve Jaekel, who were in the same predicament. A stroke of luck put us in touch with the director of the Waikiki Aquarium, a Mr. Spencer Tinker. All three of us would get free rooms inside the aquarium if we agreed to work and do some chores for the aquarium. The so-called "rooms" were really just cubbyholes with a cot. Some were like living in a tree house, two were like broom closets, and one was just some boards laid across the top of a shark tank!

My room was a real room with a real door, but I had to share it with the aquarium's huge air compressor, which ran 24 hours a day. It was so loud I couldn't hear myself think, but I somehow got used to it and managed to study and sleep in there--PING, PING, PING, PING--24 hours a day! That may be the cause of my deafness today...?

Anyway, after two weeks of "pinging", one of the students moved out, and I got his room--one of the broom closets. Actually, it was pretty nice. It was private, had a big fan, a cot, shelves, and I could almost stand up in there. I did share the space with some Moray eels, but they were very quiet. However, just outside was a large pool with seals, dolphins, and sea turtles. One of the Monk seals like to bark at night, which was disturbing, but I could turn the big fan up which drowned out the noise.

I lived there for an entire semester and really enjoyed it. The location could not have been more beautiful--right on the beach in Waikiki's Kapiolani Park next to the Kodak Center. Living there was entirely free as long as we did some off hours duties like turning on the outside lights, answering the phone, and feeding some the sea life that ate only at night. And there were fringe benefits. There was a complete kitchen with a walk-in freezer, a big refrigerator, 2 large bathrooms with showers, and a large library.

There were 6 of us students and we got along very well. At night we would sometimes spear some of the fish, crabs, and lobsters right out of their tanks and have a delicious meal of fresh seafood. The day shift never missed them! Also, we could thaw out some of the frozen tuna that was food for the seals, and cook it or eat it raw as sashimi.

Chapter 17

FIRST SEMESTER

Part 2

Sometimes I would go spear fishing with one of the other students. We would walk most the way in waist deep water to the edge of the reef--several hundred yards--where the reef plunged into the deep ocean. We had masks and snorkels--no scuba gear. The water was really cold off the reef, and there were huge coral heads and sea fans. It was beautiful but dangerous. If we didn't time the tide correctly, it was very difficult to get back on the reef. At low tide, waves would begin crashing on to the reef, and we risked getting cuts from the sharp coral. That happened to me once and that was the last time I dove the reef. I was totally exhausted, bleeding and shivering when I finally got back.

The only thing I ever speared was an octopus about 2 feet long. He/she was justifiably mad and squirted a high velocity jet of water straight into my eyes. I brought it back to the aquarium, steamed it, and ate it. It was like eating a tough, fishy inner tube...in fact, an inner tube probably would have tasted better!

Dick Conner and I bought a 1956 Buick for $65. We used it to get to the University, which was several miles away. In 1966, the University of Hawaii was a very liberal school. I'm sure it still is. The Vietnam War was very unpopular, and every Wednesday, there was a silent protest called a "Silent Vigil". At noon, students would hold hands, forming a continuous line all across the campus. But some demonstrations were more violent and students got arrested by the campus police. I remember one incident in which a student was arrested for making a US flag out of cardboard, but instead of stars, he put dollar signs. That made the national news.

President Johnson and Ladybird came to the campus while I was there. They got out of their limo right in front of me. LBJ gave a speech and Ladybird planted a tree.

Classes at UH were very informal. Some girls actually came to class wearing bikinis. Everyone wore flip-flops. The students were from all over the world and you could meet just about any ethnic type at the International Center on campus.

I met a Korean girl named Theresa and we became close friends. She was a botany major and we went everywhere together, driving around the island of Oahu in the Buick, seeing the sights.

Chapter 17

First Semester

Part 3

One afternoon Theresa and I stopped on the windward (east) side of the island for a swim at Macapu Beach. Little did we know, that while we were on the beach, we were being robbed! Some thieves broke into the trunk of my car and got all of our cash, which was only a few dollars. We later learned that Macapu was notorious for local thugs breaking into parked cars.

Another time we were sitting on the seawall outside the aquarium watching the sunset. Some other students were with us. I said to them, "Hey, what's that over there on the beach? I've never noticed that rock before". It was about 100 ft. away and no one was paying any attention to it. Finally, I got really curious and walked over to it. It was not a rock. It was a body of a surfer who had washed up on the beach. I thought he was dead, so I grabbed his arms and pulled him further up onto the sand. I turned him over on his stomach and started trying to resuscitate him the old fashion way that I had learned in Boy Scouts. To my surprise, he came to and started spitting water and coughing. By this time someone had called the police and a cop arrived within a few minutes. He started mouth to mouth, and the surfer started coming around. Finally, an ambulance arrived and took the poor man to the hospital. The news media was also there and wanted to talk to me, so I gave them some statements. The story came out in the newspaper the next day: the surfer, a native Hawaiian, had died in the hospital. He had been found by a tourist.

In 1966, the movie "Hawaii" had just been filmed. The square-rigged whaling ship used in the movie was moored at a marina north of Waikiki. One afternoon I decided to ride up and look at it. I started talking to a man painting one side of the ship. He said that the movie company, in order to save money, only paid to have one side of the ship painted, and made sure that side always appeared in the movie. He was painting the other side, so that both sides were covered. The ship was later moved to a whaling museum in Lahina on Maui.

I did not do too well academically at the University of Hawaii. I made B's in my oceanography classes but flunked calculus...again! I had already flunked it twice at the University of Alabama! I hated that stuff, but it was a required course. Does anyone really use it? Heck no. Computers do all heavy lifting now days. By the way, one of my classmates in oceanography was Robert Ballard. The world knows him as the famous explorer who discovered the "Titanic".

Chapter 18

"Gilligan"

After completing my first semester of grad school at the University of Hawaii, I returned to Mobile. I had a summer job lined up with Texaco Oil Co. in Jackson, Miss. The job was with a seismic oil exploration crew. Upon graduation from the University of Alabama with a B.S. in Geology, Texaco had offered me a full time job in New Orleans, but I turned it down in order to attend grad school in the study of oceanography. My summer job was to be a rodman for the surveyor and to cut brush along the seismic line or 'jug line'. Texaco also hired an undergraduate geology student from Boston College. His name was Steve Cassiani from Brookline, Massachusetts. As summer help, Steve and I had the same duties. We were to alternate as rodman and brush cutter.

The full time company crew was made up of men from the swamps of lower Louisiana--genuine Cajun 'coonasses'. There was also a contract crew made up of local laborers to cut brush and trees along the seismic line. They were white, uneducated back woodsy folks, used to hard work as pulpwood cutters. The job location was mostly on National Forest land south of Jackson, and we all rode to and from the job in several trucks.

I got off on the wrong foot the very first workday. I was assigned to Louis Frioux, the head surveyor, and I was to rod for him that day. He seemed friendly enough but it took me a while to get used to his thick Cajun accent. He was always saying, "Talk about, man...talk about!", when he agreed with something that was said. Anyway, when we arrived at the site, Louis got out of the truck and was setting up his tripod on the side of a dirt road. He told me to drive the truck to the first survey stake and hold up the stadia rod. Just as I got in the truck, Louis bent over to adjust the tripod and his brand new prescription sunglasses fell out of his pocket. But I was already rolling--right over his sunglasses with the front tire!

I heard all this cussing as I drove on, but didn't know at the time what Louis was so mad about. It didn't take me long to learn that Cajuns don't 'forgive and forget'! From then on Louis was on my case. I could do nothing right as far as he was concerned.

Cutting brush and vines with a heavy brush axe in stifling heat, dodging copperheads, getting stung by yellow-jackets, and putting up with those backwoods 'hayseeds' was always preferable to rodding for Louis, and I dreaded the days I had to work with him.

The contact crew was actually a pretty jovial bunch, and they took a liking to me. When they found out I was going to college in 'Hawawya', they started calling me 'Gilligan', who was a character in a popular TV series back then called "Gilligan's Island". They said that I looked like him since I was skinny and wore an old white canvas hat every day. So for the rest of the summer, I was known as 'Gilligan'.

Steve Cassiani was tall, fair-skinned and very smart. He had never been in the Deep South before and was taken aback by the crew's Cajun and Southern accents. He would ask me, "why do they say 'them' things instead of 'those' things"...and use the past perfect tense, I 'seen' him, instead of the past tense, I 'saw' him?". Of course Steve himself had a very pronounced Boston accent. He talked like a Kennedy; in fact, he said that while in high school, he had met JFK. But Steve did his job without complaining and got along fine with the crews.

The job was 5 days a week, so we didn't have much to do on the weekend. At night, we would cruise downtown Jackson in my '61 Plymouth, and would end up at a local club known as the Wagon Wheel. One night after a few beers, we were headed back to our rooming house when a car sped around us forcing me to leave the road. As I swerved, I blew my horn with a long 'beeeeeeeep!' I pulled back on the highway and proceeded on until coming to a traffic light at a busy intersection. The light was red. As we waited, I noticed an old car over on the median and a rough looking guy, getting out with a machete. He walked up to my car, hollering something, as I rolled up the window and glanced at the light, hoping it would change.
"Who are you?", I said.

"I'm the son of a b..... you blew your horn at".

"Well, I blew my horn 'cause you cut us off", I replied, still waiting for the light. I could see that he was drunk and wanted to fight.

Steve was not saying a word and was just staring straight ahead. At that moment the light changed to green and Steve shouted "GO!" and we took off. In the rear view mirror, I could see our tormentor running for his car. He chased us at high speeds for several miles, but after making turns and taking some back streets, we finally lost him.

Another memorable weekend was the 'James Meredith March', the civil rights leader who had been wounded by a gunshot while trying to register at the University of Mississippi. There was a huge group of civil rights sympathizers, including many celebrities, marching from Granada, Mississippi to the capital building in Jackson, and Steve and I were in town to watch the show. The streets were lined with National Guard soldiers, many police and state troopers, and also quite a few KKK members. As the marchers approached into town, we recognized some of the leaders. There was Martin Luther King Jr., James Meredith with a bandaged arm, Ralph Abernathy, and many other prominent, black civil rights promoters.

When the marchers reached the capital, most of them just collapsed on the lawn, tired and weary from the long march. Martin Luther King Jr. began giving a short speech. I remember him saying, "I know you've all heard us talk about 'Black Power', but what we need now is 'Green Power'", and after the speech, a hat was passed around for donations! In spite of the KKK's presence and some vocal agitators, the day passed without incidence, but Steve and I knew we were witnessing something historic.

Now, getting back to the summer job, the long hot days of 'jug line' work were dragging on. One afternoon as we were returning to Jackson, Louis had been harassing me about this and that. He was riding in the front seat and I was in the back seat of the Suburban. All of a sudden, Louis reached back, grabbed my hat off my head and threw it out of the truck, and then began laughing. I couldn't believe that he had done that and I slapped him pretty hard on the side of his face. At that, Louis was enraged. He jumped over the front seat into the back seat, but I jumped into the cargo area where all the brush axes and equipment were. Louis followed and we fought each other as we rolled around in that confined space. The party boss, Don Berson, immediately pulled over and pulled Louis off of me. Neither of us were hurt, and Don went back to retrieve my hat.

The next day Louis was his usual annoying self. This time we were riding in the back of a 4 x 4 powerwagon, on a muddy road when Louis again threw my hat off into the mud. In retaliation, I grabbed his hat and threw it. Well, we went at it again, tussling on the floor of the truck. Again, Don broke us up and said, "Look, y'all have been at it this whole summer. We're gonna settle this right now. Louis, you and Gilligan are gonna have it out over there under that tree! The rest of us are gonna' watch!" I did not back down even though I knew it was probably going to be a 'slaughter'. Even though we were the same height, Louis was tough. He was 10 years older and out weighed me by about 20 pounds or so.

As Don started to drive over to the tree, the truck got stuck in the mud. It had a winch on the bumper, so the crew began pulling the cable out and hooked it to the tree where the 'fight' was to occur. But as the winch was tightened up, there was a loud pop. The cable broke and snapped back, hitting Louis in the head, knocking him to the ground. He was bleeding a little and had a big knot on his forehead. Well, thankfully, this took the 'fight' out of him, so the big event under the tree was called off. In fact, it never did happen. A few days later, which was my last day on the job, Louis said, "Come on Gilligan, let's take a ride". I didn't know what he was up to, but got in the truck. He had a six pack of beer on ice inside..."Have a beer, man".

As we drank the beer, Louis mellowed somewhat and I realized he was trying to make amends. Then he said, "You know what your problem was when you came on this job?"

"No, what was that", I asked.

"Arrogance!" he exclaimed. "But you turned out all right, and I going to' miss dat, ya know".

"Talk about, man...talk about!" I said, trying to sound Cajun.

John Craig Shaw

Epilog: Recently, I decided to Google search Steve Cassiani. After graduating with a M.S. in geophysics, I found out that he became one of the top CEO 's of Exxon-Mobil. He was head of their exploration department, retiring last May 2009. I tried to contact him via e-mail but, so far, have not gotten a reply.

Chapter 19

SECOND SEMESTER, 1966-67

In Sept. 1966, I had just finished a summer part
time job with Texaco Oil in Mississippi, and was
undecided whether to take a full time job with Texaco
or go back to graduate school at the University
of Hawaii in Honolulu, where I had completed one
semester in oceanography.

Meanwhile, my old college friend, James Williams,
had just graduated from the University of Alabama,
and had been accepted to grad school in Hawaii,
studying ground water geology.

I decided to join Williams and go back to school.
Together we bought a '57 Ford station wagon from
our geology professor at UA--Dr. Hooks. We drove
from Alabama to California, almost non-stop. The
first night, we made it all the way to San Antonio,
just a few blocks from the Alamo.

Speeding across the southwest, we made a detour
to the famous Meteor Crater. It was late in the
afternoon, near closing time, but we paid admission
and went on down into the bottom of the crater. We
looked around a while, but when we got back to the

top, the gate was locked! The museum had closed for the day. There was no way to climb over the bars, and we thought we were going to have to wait until the next morning to get out.

A little while later, we saw someone outside the gate. It was the night watchman. We hollered, shook the gate, and finally got his attention. He had a key and gladly let us out.

We had planned to sell the car in Los Angeles and fly on to Hawaii. Arriving in L.A., we pulled into a used car lot.

"I'll give you 75 for it", said the salesman. We had paid $395 to Dr. Hooks.

"75 dollars?" we asked. "Is that all?"

"No, not 75 dollars...75 CENTS!" replied the salesman. "You've got an Alabama tag, a George Wallace sticker on the back window, and no registration! The state of Alabama does not require registration, but California does, which means I cannot legally sell this car here. Sorry guys", he said.

Having very little money between us, selling the car was critical. Luckily, my great-grandmother Willborn and Aunt lived close by in Hemet, and graciously bailed us out, buying the car for $395!

Arriving in Hawaii, we had trouble finding a suitable place to live. I tried to get back in the Waikiki Aquarium, where I had lived the previous semester, but it was full (6 students). We finally rented a couple of rooms in a run-down home of an elderly Japanese woman. This did not work out--too many roaches! We moved a couple more times, finally moving to a new apartment building in a nice neighborhood.

Used cars were very cheap in Honolulu, and there was a surplus of them. We bought a '54 Plymouth convertible for $100. It was a great car, and we named it "Melrose", which was the name of the street that my great grandmother lived on back in Hemet... remember, she bought our old station wagon!

My subjects that semester were Physical Oceanography, German, and Calculus. I had flunked calculus during the previous semester, so had to retake it. I hated it!

James had met an interesting female student from Nepal, and said he was going to try to date her. She was very shy and not at all used to dating, since it was her custom to be formerly chaperoned by her parents who were in Nepal. After a while, they started studying together...and dating...and about a year later, got married. But that's another story.

By Christmas break, we had 2 weeks off from class. James and I decided to take a flight to some of the other islands. We flew to the big island (Hawaii) and to Maui. We rented a car in Hawaii and toured the whole island. We were too broke to afford a room, so we had to sleep in the car. This trip is further detailed in another chapter (Christmas Trip).

When we got back to Honolulu, I happened to meet up with an old childhood friend, Jimmy Eveland. He and I had grown up on the same street in Westlawn in Mobile. On a whim, he had taken a flight to the islands, where he planned to go "hippie". He moved in with us for a short time and said that he was trying to get rid of all his material "wealth"! He had given away his bicycle and nearly everything he owned, but kept just essential clothes and personal gear. I think he kept his toothbrush!

Chapter 20

Christmas Trip, 1966

With two weeks off (Christmas vacation) before finals during my second semester at UH, roommate James Williams and I decided to visit Maui and Hawaii (the Big Island). We booked a flight from Honolulu to the Kona Coast on Hawaii. We boarded the plane and found our seats. As we sat down, a large man in an Aloha shirt got on, and began walking down the aisle. We immediately recognized him as Richard Boone of "Have Gun Will Travel", a popular TV series back in the 60's. He sat in the seat directly across from us. With his pockmarked complexion, he was really mean looking and glared at us as he pulled out his newspaper and began reading. We decided not to strike up a conversation with him for fear that he might pull a small derringer on us! A few weeks later we understood why he was going to the Big Island, because the orange juice commercial that he made in Kona was all over TV.

Arriving in Kona, we rented a compact car and started touring the island. We saw all the sights including Kilauea National Park, waterfalls, rain forests, the Parker Ranch, Hilo, the sea cliffs, and the place where Captain Cook was killed. We slept in the car and used public restrooms.

I had been given an address by a Mobile friend who was in the Pacific during World War Two. My friend Roy Eveland, who at the time was an FBI agent in Mobile, had told me to look up two elderly ladies that took care of him while in Hawaii. I don't remember their names, but they lived in an old Victorian home somewhere in the interior and not far from the huge volcano, Mauna Kea. We found the home and knocked on the door. The two ladies were there, and in spite of our appearance, said to come in. The house was like a museum, full of beautiful antique furniture. When I told them that I was a friend of Roy's, they were overjoyed, and said we must take tea with them! We had tea and they talked about Roy and the war. They invited us to stay on, but we thanked them and pried ourselves away from their gracious hospitality and hit the road.

The next day James and I decided to climb Mauna Kea, the higher of the two main volcanoes (Elevation 13,784 ft.). It is the largest mountain on Earth when you consider its base is sitting on the floor of the deep ocean. We drove our Datsun as far up as we could, until the dirt road became a narrow trail. We parked the car and started walking. There was very little vegetation, no trees, and the climb didn't seem all that steep. So far, the trek was deserted, but soon we saw some men with rifles coming down the trail. They met us and said they were hunting wild goats.

The gentle grade was deceiving, and after a while, we began to get exhausted. James said he would meet me back at the car, and turned around. I kept going until finally I could see the summit. There was no snow, just a reddish brown peak. I was probably within a couple of hundred yards of the top, but I simply could not take another step. After taking a photo of the peak, I turned around and headed back.

Today, I guess there is a nice paved road to the top, because the summit is home to the University's Keck Observatory, a prime viewing area for astronomers.

Chapter 21

LEAVING HAWAII

The movie "Hawaii", an adaptation of James Michener's novel, was premiering at a Honolulu theater, and the three of us decided to go. The theater was packed, but we got in. Of course, being "Haolis" (Caucasians), we were in the minority. This became evident when the crowd cheered and clapped when the White missionaries were killed!

In a week or two, Eveland went back to the mainland, leaving James and I struggling with final exams. James did fine, but I ended up getting a "C" in calculus, which put me on probation. You had to maintain a "B" average in grad school, and so the "C", averaged in with the "F" the previous semester, was not good. My student advisor told me that poor grades meant a strong possibility of being drafted into the military. Sure enough, I got a letter from the draft board, saying to appear in Montgomery, Alabama for an Army physical.

I had come to the conclusion that if I were going to Vietnam, it would not be in the Army. I decided to drop out of grad school and join the Navy. However, the Naval recruiter in Honolulu said that due to my poor eyesight, I was ineligible for the Navy...but that the Army would still take me! Bummer!

James, who was obligated to serve as an officer in the USAF (ROTC), also decided to drop grad school and fulfill his military obligation. So, we sold "Melrose" the car, and booked passage on a ship, the USS President Wilson, bound for San Francisco. The fare was $100 each at 'dormitory' class. That meant we would be on the lowest deck, in bunk beds with a curtain for privacy, all of us in a large open room. Our fellow "class" mates were mostly oriental men. We were allowed to dine with the second-class passengers, and walk freely about the ship. Amazingly, the Pacific was as calm as a millpond...but I still got seasick on the second day out! I recovered quickly, however, with the help of some medication from sickbay. On the fourth day, we were passing under the Golden Gate Bridge into San Francisco. We intended to buy a cheap car in Frisco and take a leisurely trip back to Alabama...which we did. We pooled our money and bought a used Peugeot for about $400, and after spending one night in a cheap hotel, headed for the Napa Valley.

In the Napa Valley, we were thrilled to learn about the FREE wine tasting stations along the way...and we took advantage of just about every one! Whoa! Stay on your side of the road, man!

There they were. The Sierra Nevada Mountains, and in March, there was still plenty of snow up there. We were hoping to get over the mountains before dark, but we didn't make it. After the Napa Valley, we were in bad need of sleep, and at some point, high in the mountains, we decided to stop and rest for the night. Thinking that a snowdrift would insulate us from the cold, we plowed the compact car head on into a snow bank! I don't know whether that helped or not, but it was still like trying to sleep in a freezer!

In the morning, it was on to Lake Tahoe and Reno, where James, always the gambler, had to stop for some poker playing. Harry James, the famous trumpeter, was playing in a small lobby, and I sat and listened until Williams returned. Back on the road through the empty Nevada desert, we camped along a dirt road and built a fire. It was still cold!

After winning a few bucks in Reno, James was smitten and wanted to try Vegas, so on we went, passing through a few old mining towns. In Las Vegas, we hit the casinos once more. James went straight to the poker room, while I went to the slots. I have never been a gambler but I was having fun with the nickel slot machines. Well, James was taken "to the cleaners" in the poker room and was ready to hit the road. I had one nickel left in change and dropped it in the slot. Jackpot!! Wow, I was rich! I had won 7 dollars in nickels!

This was a real so called "road trip", so having no particular route or deadlines to meet (my physical was a month off), we just took a more or less zigzag course across the country, stopping and seeing whatever was of interest to us. We toured Boulder Dam and the Grand Canyon. One stop that was a must was Dodge City, Kansas. We had to see Boot Hill and the Wyatt Earp Museum!

Somewhere west of Oklahoma City, our little Peugeot began losing power and making a loud hammering sound. It ran slower...and slower...and slower...until we were down to just above walking speed. Creeping into Oklahoma City, we found a service station with a mechanic. It was a burned valve, and it took just about all the money we had left to get it fixed.

Back on the road again, we headed straight for Alabama. In Mobile, James paid (or promised to pay) my half of the car, and he went home to Decatur, where he eventually fulfilled his tour of duty with the Air Force (4 years). I never took the Army physical. Instead, I joined the Air Force Reserve Unit at Brookley AFB in Mobile, serving as a cook in the mess hall.

Although our superiors said that it was just a matter of time before we would be activated to Vietnam, we never were. In fact, when LBJ became president, the base was closed, and our unit became "inactive", which meant no more meetings or summer camps until being officially discharged in 1973

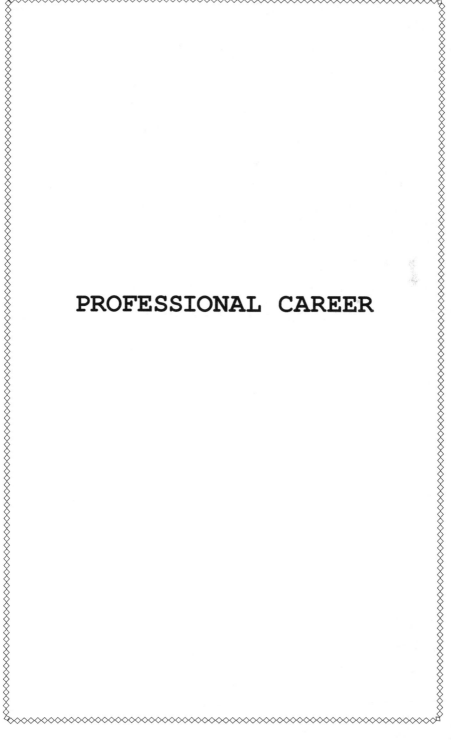

PROFESSIONAL CAREER

Chapter 22

GEIGY CHEMICAL

Part 1

When I completed my 4 months of active duty as a cook in the US Air Force Reserve, I was looking for a job. My active duty was served in the mess hall at Brookley AFB from June 1967, to Sept. My job as a cook was like 4 months of K.P. and I was looking for something on a little higher skill level.

I entered my resume with the US Government and with an employment agency, as a graduate geologist with one year of grad school in oceanography, but at the time, there was a hiring 'freeze' on federal employment. I was living with my parents in west Mobile. After a few weeks, I heard from the agency and took a job with Geigy Chemical Plant in McIntosh, Alabama as a Junior Chemist. The pay was $550 per month, which I thought was great.

The work was in the quality control lab, running all sorts of chemical tests on Geigy products--mostly insecticides and herbicides. I was on a swing shift--days, evenings, and graveyard shifts-

-changing every 7 days. McIntosh is about 45 miles from Mobile, and I joined a carpool with 4 other workers. We all had Volkswagen bugs, so it was a cozy commute!

No question about it...working at Geigy was hazardous! The fumes were terrific and some days, we were forced to wear gas masks, just to be able to breath, even though we were inside a building. The pollution was terrible, and Geigy was cited twice for 2 major fish kills caused by their effluent dumped in the Tombigbee river. It was before EPA and OSHA, so the environment and safety were not big concerns. However, we did have to submit a blood test every now and then to see how much 'product' we were accumulating.

There were only 3 chemists on the 'graveyard' shift, and one night we heard a loud siren going off just outside the lab. None of us knew what it was, so we walked outside to see what was going on. We heard a loud hissing sound, but otherwise didn't notice anything unusual. When we came back to work the next night, we learned that a valve on the hydrogen cyanide tank had failed, setting off an alarm. That was what we heard, and like idiots, we went outside where one whiff would have been enough to kill us. But no one was injured because a westerly breeze had blown the gas away from the lab. After that episode, I decided to try to find another job.

Chapter 22

GEIGY CHEMICAL

Part 2

I worked at Geigy Chemical for about 8 months before receiving 2 offers of federal employment. One offer was a GS-5 as an Oceanographer (US Coast and Geodetic Survey) in Maryland, and the second offer was a GS-7 as a geologist trainee with the Mobile District, Corps of Engineers. My father had some 'pull' with the second offer because he not only worked for the Corps, but also was in a carpool with Dick Coogan, the chief geologist. So I accepted the higher-grade offer and was hired as a geologist 'trainee' on a one-year training period instead of a permanent position, because of a federal hiring freeze at the time.

After I completed my training period, I was advanced to a permanent position as a GS-9 Geologist. I stayed with the Mobile District until January 1996, when I accepted an early retirement offer at the age of 52. Except for a 3 month consulting job with a small grouting company in Texas (1996), I have been retired ever since, living in a small cabin with a white dog named Maggie, on Fish River in Baldwin County, Alabama.

Most of the next series of stories occurred during my career with the Corps.

Chapter 23

CORPS OF ENGINEERS

My one-year training period with the Corps of Engineers was a mixed bag. I spent time in the Mobile District office and some time with field personnel where I received valuable training with other Corps geologists, core drill crews, engineers and technicians on various construction projects. I particularly enjoyed working outdoors with the drill crews and was reluctant to go back to the office in Mobile.

The year of training went by quickly and soon, as a GS-9, I was sent directly to work as a field geologist at Bankhead Lock and Dam where core drilling was underway for a new and larger lock system. The lock and dam is a few miles west of Birmingham, Alabama on the Black Warrior River.

The chief geologist had warned me about the "wild" nature of the core drill crews. That proved to be the case with most of them. There was a lot of hard drinking, carousing, bar brawling, and late night poker playing. I had not been on the job long before a night of boozing resulted in a fatal car accident of one of the drillers.

On many occasions I wound up partying along with them on jobs all over the country. And sometimes they wouldn't take no for an answer. I remember one late night on a job in Sedalia, Missouri when I was awakened by loud knocks on my door: "Hey Shaw...get up...let's go have a beer...it's Jack's birthday!" It was Jack de Bardelaben, Jerry Bullard, and James Wyatt--drunk as skunks! I told them no, I was going back to sleep and locked the door. After climbing back in bed, I heard a rattling of the motel window and the sound of the window being raised. One of them grabbed my feet and pulled me through the window to the outside!

I held them off long enough to get dressed, and away we went to the motel lounge. More crews were inside (feeling no pain) and after another round of beers, the waitress brought out a small cake covered with white icing and one burning candle stuck in it. She set it down in front of Jack who blew out the candle and got ready to indulge. He took a big bite of the cake and immediately spit it out, throwing the whole cake to the floor with a splat! Old Jack, being good-natured and comical, was often the brunt of a joke. The "cake" was really a very large half of a white onion covered in white icing!

The next morning--bright and early--we were definitely feeling pain!

Chapter 24

LAND OF OZ

Part 1

The project was a joint venture of several federal agencies, to explore and test a potential site for a nuclear waste repository--in other words, a "tomb" to store radioactive waste.

As a field geologist with the Mobile District, I was sent to the site near Lyons, Kansas to assist other geologists, scientists, engineers, and drill crews (also with the Mobile District) on a so-called "secret" project for the Atomic Energy Commission. The year was 1970 and the work was to drill two core borings through several hundred feet of a salt (halite) formation, in hopes that this thick bed of inert material could be utilized as a repository. Central Kansas is known for salt mining. At the time, the Morton and Sterling Companies owned deep underground mines nearby. Those companies had excavated huge quantities of commercial grade salt, leaving large tunnels and rooms within the salt formation.

Besides the Atomic Energy Commission and the Corps, there were the U.S. Geological Survey and various consultants from the private sector, including Schlumberger well logging service.

As for the project being "secret", that was a joke. Everyone in town, from the motel clerk to the Dairy Queen waitresses seemed to know more about the job than we did! Soon after arriving at my motel, I was met by a newspaper reporter who wanted to interview me. I guess it was about the biggest event to hit that part of Kansas since "Wizard of Oz"! The locals were especially intrigued by the southern drawl of the Alabama core drill crews. They became a major attraction, and a big hit with the ladies--one driller later married one.

The drilling finally got started and continued around the clock--two 12-hour shifts for several months. I was on the night shift. The coring of the evaporite rock was done with a long core barrel, which extracted a 20-foot length of 6-inch diameter core with each pull. The rock was very heavy, and I had to log, photograph, and wrap in plastic sheeting, every inch of it. Stored in wooden boxes, the core was eventually sent to the Oak Ridge Lab in Tennessee for further testing.

After completing the first boring, which was drilled to a depth of 1,000 feet, there was some down time while the drill rig was set up on the second hole. In the meantime the Corps decided to send me on another Atomic Energy Comm. project at the Lab in Oak Ridge, Tenn. where I was to log core for another Mobile drill crew. Since I was the only field geologist the Mobile District had at the time, I was to monitor the two projects simultaneously. That meant flying back and forth from Kansas to Tennessee every so many days.

Well, after many weeks of commuting from job to job, I finally got a chance to fly home to Mobile for a long weekend. First, I had to drive to Wichita to catch a 1 am flight...and it started snowing... and the snow became a blizzard! Everything was white. Creeping along at about 15 mph, the only way I could tell I was still on the highway was to stay between the fencerows. But somehow, I slipped and slid into the Wichita airport by nightfall. I got my ticket, ate supper, and sat around awaiting my flight. All the while, it continued to snow.

Finally, it was time for my flight, and who should appear at the gate, but the pilot himself. The Braniff Boeing 707 was out on the runway waiting for me and two other passengers to board. It was still snowing, and I really got nervous when the pilot took out a flashlight and said, "Come on you brave souls and follow me!" We followed him out onto the dark tarmac.

We boarded by the rear ramp, which was lowered from the plane. Except for the aisle lights, it was dark inside, and I took an aisle seat at the very rear of the plane. Looking around I saw that the flight was full, and most of the passengers were asleep. Since the plane was already on the runway, all we had to do was take off. The engines revved up, and we started to pick up speed when I heard, "STOP... STOP...STOP the PLANE!" It was the stewardess yelling as she ran up the aisle to the pilots' cabin. Then I saw what the problem was. The boarding ramp was still down, dragging along the runway!

Just before liftoff, the jet slowed back down and finally stopped. The stewardess came back, cussing like a sailor. Since I was in the last row of seats, I jumped up and helped her raise the ramp and lock it. So off we went again--this time with no problems. Amazingly, most of the passengers had slept through the whole ordeal; however, a young soldier across the aisle from me was just waking up.

"What town was that back there?" he asked me.

"That was Wichita, Kansas", I replied. Immediately, tears began running down his face, and I asked him what was wrong. He was sobbing by this time and said, "I was supposed to change planes there to go home to Oklahoma City! I left Vietnam two days ago, and I've been flying ever since...now I missed my flight!" After hearing his story, I was almost in tears myself.

Well, I went back to where the stewardess was sitting and told her the soldier's story. She said maybe there was something that could be done, and walked up to the captain's cabin. A few minutes later, I felt the plane banking to the left...we were headed for Oklahoma City!

Yep, it was an unscheduled landing and a slight delay, but one U.S. soldier was ever so grateful. And Braniff Airlines, a wild and crazy company, moved up a few notches in my book!

Chapter 25

SALT MINE

After a week end in Mobile, Alabama, I returned to the "salt mine" in Lyons, Kansas. The drilling on the second borehole was still underway. The around the cock shift work dragged on, and everyone began to get weary, especially the drill crews.

One night on my shift, the crew showed up a little "tipsy". The drilling supervisor was off that night, and it was just the three-man drill crew and myself on the job. It was a chilly night so we lit the salamander (a diesel burning heater), and the driller lowered the core barrel and drill stem to the bottom of the hole. As the coring began, the two helpers went to the pickup. They came back with a guitar and a large cooler full of "Old Milwaukee"! I couldn't resist the ice-cold brew, so we sat around the salamander as one of the crew began plunkin' a tune.

After the second or third round of refreshments, the guitar plunker looked at me and said, "How 'bout it Doc...play us a little "Wildwood Flower". I played a few tunes, and we all started singing along. The core barrel was in anhydrite, which is a very hard rock, so there wasn't much to do but party on. Well, that went on for another hour or so, and then we settled down...just listening to the steady roar of the drill rig.

Hypothetically...an owl, flying overhead that cold clear night, would have seen a lit up drill rig in the midst of a cutover milo field, and four men, lying on the ground near a glowing heater... and quite a few Old Milwaukee cans littering the surrounding area.

The next thing I remember was being shaken awake and seeing Bill Lambert, the drilling supervisor, standing over us. It was about 4 am and Bill was ranting and cussing, kicking beer cans, and shaking his head.

"G--D-- it! I cain't leave you guys fo ah G--D-- minute! Git up and clean up this G--D-- mess! Yuhimmy nah?"

Bill Lambert was a typical drilling supervisor, also known as a "tool pusher". Most tool pushers had been drillers themselves, but were upgraded to be supervisors because of their loud, overbearing personalities--sort of like a drill sergeant.

****

A few days later, I had a meeting with one of the other Corps geologists on the day shift. His name was Mike Green and we were going over our geologic reports in his hotel room. Mike was from another District. He was "clean-cut" and had a reputation for going strictly "by the book"...and that did not set well with Bill Lambert.

Hey Shaw, let me ask you something", said Mike. "Every time I talk to Bill, he always says this word at the end of every sentence. It's kind of like a chant, and it sounds like 'yuhimmy nah'. What the heck does that mean?" I laughed and knew exactly what Mike was referring to. Bill was really saying "Do you hear me now?" which is like saying "Do you understand?" But in Bill's backwoods drawl, it came out "yuhimmy nah?"

Mike also told me that the drill crew had threatened to throw him in the mud sump when the job was over. A few weeks later, as the job was winding down, Mike somehow ended up in the mud sump...
yuhimmy nah?

***

Epilog: The Lyons, Kansas, nuclear waste repository was never built.

Chapter 26

EMERGENCY LANDING

I guess it was bound to happen. On one of the many flights from Kansas to Tennessee to monitor the two jobs, there was flight scare.

For some reason I was routed through Chicago instead of my usual direct flight. I made my connection at O'Hare Airport and boarded an Eastern 707 for a night flight to Knoxville. After a short while in the air, the plane went through some unusual gyrations. Moments later, the captain said, "Ladies and gentlemen, we have a problem with the aircraft... the airbrakes don't seem to be functioning and we need the airbrakes to land. Please buckle your safety belts up good, because I'm going to try some extreme maneuvering to try to get the brakes unstuck".

The next few minutes the pilot flew the 707 like it was a fighter jet! We made sudden turns, banking left and right, then up and down...went into a rather steep dive, and then leveled off.

The Captain: "Well, it didn't work. The brakes are still stuck, so I'm afraid we can't land in

Knoxville. I have asked for an emergency landing in Atlanta, which has one of the longest runways in the world. I just want to tell you that this has happened to me once before, and the plane made a safe landing...so just try to relax. By the way, the bar is open at no charge!"

Most of the passengers remained calm, but the alcohol began to flow. I ordered a double martini... the first one I ever had and it did help!

The weather was perfectly clear, and we finally approached the Atlanta airport.

The Captain: "Well folks, we are cleared to make an emergency landing. I don't want you to be afraid, but since we have no airbrakes, we will hit the runway at flying speed. I will try to set 'er down as close to the start of the runway as possible, so we can get the full benefit of the pavement to slow us down. The runway has been foamed and emergency crews are standing by. See you on the ground".

Of course after that little speech, everyone was either terrified, passed out, or just numb!

The pilot was right about the landing. We hit the runway at the same speed we had been flying, and I have never seen buildings go by so fast! The brakes on the tires burned up almost immediately, but I don't think we had any blowouts. I was at a window seat, so I could see the fire trucks and emergency personnel as we streaked by. I didn't think we were ever going to stop...and we didn't!

As we got to the end of the runway, the plane made an abrupt turn to the left, which caused the wing tip to scrape the pavement, sending out sparks.

We were then on another runway or ramp, but at last, we were beginning to slow down. The passengers broke from our silence and began clapping and cheering as we rode along at a smooth, regular speed.

We must have traveled quite a distance from the terminal, because it seemed like a long time before we finally got to the gate.
When we came to a stop, the captain came back over the intercom..."Welcome to Atlanta folks...Whew!"

Eastern Airlines paid for meals and lodging for any passengers laid-over in Atlanta. I got booked on another flight to Knoxville that same night with a story to tell the drill crew the next morning!

Chapter 27

CALYX HOLE

Part 1

The Tennessee Tombigbee Waterway was a huge undertaking, probably the largest project ever done by the Corps of Engineers. I was involved with this project as a field geologist for approximately 10 years. I was in charge of many drill crews and soil technicians. Most of the work involved taking core (rock) and soil samples at each of the ten lock and dam sites, monitoring ground water, and drilling water wells for aquifer tests. My main job, along with other field geologists, was to log the core and write up field logs, which were sent to the office in Mobile.

Various engineering tests were done at the South Atlantic Division Lab in Marietta, Georgia. All this was done to locate a suitable foundation for the locks and dams.

One of the first lock and dam sites to be drilled out was the Aliceville Lock and Dam in 1970. Aliceville was the closest large town but the actual site was near Pickensville, Alabama--a small community in Pickens County.

John MacFadyen, the other field geologist, and I kept noticing some very soft clay seams in the core of the Eutaw Formation. These seams were of major concern to Dick Coogan, the chief geologist. It was thought that these soft seams might have been caused by the drilling process, but if they were indeed natural layers in the rock, well, that could cause a structural failure in the foundation.

After several meetings with other geologists and engineers, it was decided to drill what is known as a calyx hole. A calyx hole is a large diameter (36" to 42") boring drilled into the foundation rock. A geologist can then be lowered down inside to closely observe and log the rock in its natural state. That was going to be my job.

The drill rig was brought in and 42 inch steel casing was set to 33 feet, sealing off the soft soil layer (overburden). Three dewatering wells were drilled around the calyx boring in order to prevent ground water from flooding the hole as it was drilled. The driller, Johnny Cooper, began coring with a large diameter core barrel, cutting 5 feet of rock at a time. After cutting the initial 5 feet, a man was lowered down to break up the rock, put it in a bucket which was pulled back up to the surface. This procedure was painstakingly slow and dangerous.

After advancing the boring to about 40 feet of depth, it was decided to continue the drilling using a "bucket auger". This method eliminated the need to send a man down to "muck out" the chunks of rock. The bucket auger scooped up the rock cuttings as it was turned, and then was pulled up and dumped. The boring was finally drilled to a depth of 90 feet below ground. I should say that the so called "rock" of the Eutaw Formation is not really rock, but layers of hardened clay and compact sand. There was no casing set in that zone. The only thing preventing the hole from caving in were the dewatering wells, which were pumping continuously, 24 hours a day.

Well, it was then time for someone to be lowered down to the bottom in order to check out the condition of the boring. This was usually done by the driller, but Cooper refused to go down. "I ain't about to go down in that damn thing!" said he. None of the helpers volunteered either. I had been in a couple of calyx borings before, but they were drilled in hard rock, not soft material like this. So I also refused to go down and went to the phone to call the office.

"Aw, go on down in there and do your job! I've been in many calyx holes and never had any problems", said Coogan.

"No Sir", I said. "I'm not going in there. The driller won't even go down!"

So Coogan said he was going to send Pete Dyer up to take a look. Pete, in his sixties, was a very experienced soil and rock technician, who had done just about every kind of fieldwork known, and had been with the Corps many years. When old Pete arrived, he didn't even hesitate. He stepped in the bucket with a flashlight and was lowered to the bottom--ninety feet down!

Chapter 27

CALYX HOLE

Part 2

After Pete was pulled back up to the surface, he convinced me that it was safe, and I prepared to go down. Donning rain gear and hardhat, I took the flashlight, and climbed in the boson's chair, giving the signal to lower away. When I got below the steel casing at depth 33 ft., I probed at the sides of the "rock" wall. The clay seemed sound, but when I descended into the lower portion of the hole, I was amazed at how loose the sand layers were. Sand was sloughing off as I went further down. At the bottom (90 ft.), looking up, all I could see was a small circle of light.

Logging the boring was not easy. Water was constantly dripping down, so I could not write in my logbook. Also, I had an electric light with a long cord in one hand, and being wet, it gave me some mild shocks! I ended up having to shout up to Pete, who wrote down what I was seeing below. This took many hours, and I had to go in and out many times.

When I completed the log, the Corps sent up a crowd of folks to observe the boring. Office engineers and geologists, including Dick Coogan and Jack Bryan, came to the site, as well as the Corps' chief geologist from Washington D.C. I had observed some of the soft clay seams in question, so others wanted to go down to verify what I had logged. They came up, satisfied that the soft seams were natural and not caused by drilling.

The next day, after all the visitors had left, it was time to backfill and grout up the calyx hole. The generator running the dewatering pumps was shut off and finally, it was quiet. It had been running steadily for at least a week. Immediately, we started hearing rumbling and splashing from down below. The hole was caving in. We were shocked at how quickly this occurred, and realized that if the generator had suddenly quit running while someone was in the hole, well...that still gives me "the willies"!

Chapter 28
"Short Boy"

Core Drillers--Tenn-Tom Project

During my work with the Corps of Engineers, there was never a more colorful group of characters than the Mobile District's core drill crews. Most of them were from small towns in the Montgomery area--like Wetumpka, Prattville, Shorter, Millbrook, Tallassee, Booth, and Clanton. What they lacked in education, they made up for in brute strength, stamina, and down-home ingenuity.

They understood motors and machinery. When operating a drill rig, their movements-- shifting gears, pulling levers, turning knobs, etc.-- were so fast, it was almost like watching a dance routine! And timing was crucial or someone could get seriously hurt.

At night, most of them were heavy drinkers, while a few were teetotalers.
They had a colorful way of talking and could impersonate each other, and also some of their bosses in Mobile. Cuss words were the norm, but a few never even said as much as a "darn". They had nicknames such as "Wheel", "Double-knit", "Hound Dog", "Foots", "DeBar", "Knowledge", "Jitterbug", "Red", and "NoKnox". My nickname was "Doc", or sometimes "Doctor"
Shaw.

In the early Tenn-Tom years, most of the crews were white. During the late '70s, there were a few black helpers hired. This caused some friction for a while, especially with the "old timers" who had a habit of calling all new helpers "Short Boy".

I was working with a crew at the Aliceville site, when one of the newly hired black helpers came on the job. He was a college student and his name was Ed. All that day the driller, instead of calling him by name, called him "Short Boy". This went on for several days until the helper became annoyed and finally confronted the driller.

"Look", he said, "My name is Ed or Eddie!
I don't want to be called "Short Boy" any more. You call me by my name, Ed or Eddie!"

From then on, for the rest of the Summer, the drillers called him "ED-or-EDDIE"...not just Ed or just Eddie...it was always run together: "ED-or-EDDIE"!

Chapter 29

MONSTER BEAVER DAM

Part 1

Long before the Tennessee-Tombigbee Waterway became a reality in the mid 1980's, there were years of site selection studies for locks and dams, many miles of surveying, and thousands of core and soil samples taken--all by Corps of Engineer field crews--in some of the deepest woods and muddiest swamps of the southeast.

It's easy enough for engineers to study a map and say, "We need to drill some borings at these locations", but there were sometimes monumental difficulties when the field crews were confronted with the task of actually moving heavy equipment to those locations.

Surveyors did the first task. They cut survey lines into the site area, and laid out the project configuration, and spotted the stakes where borings were to be drilled.

I remember one of the swampiest (and snakiest)

site locations was in Pool "D", which was between Lock "D" and Lock "E" or about 10 miles north of Fulton, Mississippi.

It was a hot Summer morning when Doug Jones (soil technician) and I met a survey party, who were to show us where they had laid out the stakes. We were all dressed in hip waders because we knew we were going into a swamp. The lead surveyor had a pistol, loaded with rat shot bullets. It was snake season, and, for some reason, cottonmouths were extremely plentiful in the Lock "D"/Pool "D" area. We started in along one of the survey lines, and had not gone very far into the swamp when water was already over our waders.

Suddenly, the leader stopped and pointed out a medium sized cottonmouth. Drawing his pistol, he shot but only wounded it, and the snake slithered into the muddy water. By this time, the water was waist deep, and we knew there was a very mad moccasin somewhere near. I held my breath as I followed the others, halfway expecting to feel a pair of fangs sink into my upper thigh. As we got further in, the water got shallower. We emptied our water soaked waders and proceeded onward. Then we started seeing more snakes. They were everywhere... on logs, hanging on limbs, and not the least bit afraid of us! We were the intruders! But just about all of them were young ones, which have a more colorful pattern than the mature ones, but can still deliver a lethal bite. There were too many of them to shoot, so we just watched very carefully where we were stepping.

Finally, we came to a prominent ridge, which stretched for some distance. It was a monster beaver dam, higher than our heads! It must have been 6 to 8 ft high...larger than any of us had ever seen. The surveyors knew about it and said that the stakes were on the other side of the beaver pond, and we could see where the pink flagging continued on into the swamp. The survey leader said they were going back, leaving Doug and I to find the stakes on our own. The pond was over our heads near the dam, and we had to swim a ways until we could walk in neck deep water. The pond got gradually shallower until we were again walking along the survey line and, at last, found the drill stakes. But how in the world were we going to get a drill rig in there?

Chapter 29

MONSTER BEAVER DAM

Part 2

The Mobile District Core Drill Section had a reputation of being the best in the world. Their motto was "Have Drill, Will Travel", and travel they did...from the jungles of Panama to the Alaskan wilderness...from Mount St. Helens to the African interior...from Iceland to the South Pacific...all the four corners of the world. Now they were dealing with the soft muddy swamps of the upper Tombigbee. Thanks to men like Dave Childers and Charles Cox, the drill rigs were designed to match the terrain...everything from small skid rigs, truck mounted rigs, track rigs, and swamp buggies...all used extensively on the Tenn-Tom.

"Well, we'll have to build a 'corduroy' road to them drill stakes", said Andrew Parker, one of the drill supervisors, after I showed him the location.

"A what?" I didn't know what he was talking about.

"We'll cut a trail into the site (they had decided to bypass the beaver dam by coming in from the north). Then we'll cut a bunch of them small trees and lay 'em cross-ways, until they're thick enough to drive a rig in".

The idea sounded crazy to me, but the crews went right to work on it, cutting a trail into a 'gum swamp', where trees were only a foot or two apart. The trail was several hundred yards long, and it took several days to complete the road. But when finished, I was impressed how easily the 15-ton drill rig was driven right to the stake with no trouble at all.

The borings were completed, and the beavers were able to keep their dam...at least for a year or two longer. Eventually, the Corps hired a professional beaver trapper to rid the waterway route of many a beaver. He trapped them in live traps and relocated them to other areas outside the project.

JCS

Chapter 30

OVERSEA ADVENTURE

In March of 1976, I volunteered for a 6-month assignment in Saudi Arabia. The monarchy was in the process of modernizing their country, and had contracted the US Government to design and supervise many engineering projects. Many employees from the US Army Corps of Engineers, including several from the Mobile District, were already in the country.

My assignment was to oversee the drilling of a deep-water well--a test well for a future military base (King Khalid Military City).

Before leaving Mobile, I had to have a letter from my church, proving that I was baptized in a Christian church--Jews were not allowed visas! I left the US from JFK in New York, and was on my way to Livorno, Italy, where I would be briefed about my assignment at the Mediterranean Division Headquarters (Leghorn Military Facility).

I left the US on a night flight and the 707 was packed. Half way across the Atlantic, I was awakened by loud voices nearby. A fight broke out between a man in front and a man behind me! It seemed the fight was over smoking in the 'non smoking' section. "I weel keel heem", shouted the middle easterner, to the man smoking, as he leaned over me trying to grab the cigarette. "Poot ceegaret out... poot ceegaret OUT!" Soon, a petite stewardess in a micro skirt, grabbed the middle eastern man and slung him back in his seat, and took the offending cigarette from the smoker, telling them both to sit down and shut up! All was quiet afterwards.

Before landing in Rome, we learned that there was some sort of a baggage handlers' union strike, and that we would have to circle the airport for a while. Finally, we were allowed to land. With no baggage personnel, each of the 200 plus, "jet lagged", passengers had to crawl up in the baggage compartment, to find their luggage. There was a lot of scrambling and shoving bags around. And, for some reason, the plane had stopped far out on the hot tarmac, and we had to walk to the terminal.

I had reservations for the night in a hotel in downtown Rome. After changing US dollars into lira, I caught a taxi into the city. I thought it was strange that there was no logo and no meter in the taxi. The driver could speak English and decided to take me on a tour around the city, pointing out many sights. When we finally got to my hotel, I paid for the ride with my 'new money', later realizing that I had been grossly overcharged by a "fake" taxi driver! Oh well...live and learn.

Chapter 31

TUSCANY, ITALY

I stayed in Rome for 2 days, visited the Coliseum, as well as many ruins of ancient Rome. The Corps sent a van to take me to Livorno, which is in the Tuscany Region of Italy, known for its marble quarries, and its delicious food and wine. I stayed in a hotel located right on the Mediterranean Sea, and had the best food I have ever eaten. You could not go wrong choosing a restaurant there, and the prices were very reasonable.

After the first week of briefings at Leghorn, I went on a weekend trip with 3 other geologists-- Earl Titcomb, Bill Barker, and Dave Petza. They had a rented car and after Friday's work, we headed west along the coast to Genoa, Chris Columbus's hometown. We spent the night in a cheap hostel. The next day we saw Columbus's birthplace, drove on to Cannes, France, and then on to the tiny country of Monaco.

We visited the palace...didn't see anyone we knew, like Grace Kelly, so we went to the Monte Carlo Casino and the yacht harbor. That was quite a picturesque drive, to say the least.

Continuing on we headed north into the French interior. Seeing 2 pretty young French girls, hitchhiking, we stopped and offered them a ride. There were 4 of us men in a very small compact car, so the 2 girls had to sit in our laps! They didn't seem to mind and chatted away in French, while we wondered what in the world they were saying. When we got a few miles down the road, they wanted out. We stopped, took their pictures, and left, heading on to Digne, where we spent the second night. Digne, France, was a very quaint little village in the foothills of the Alps. It looked like a storybook place. In fact, it was just that. Digne was the setting for Victor Hugo's Les Miserables!

After a great meal and beers in an old tavern, we found another hostel--an upgrade from the last one. The next morning (Sunday), we went up into the Alps, stopping at a ski lodge for a while. Then south, back across the Italian border into Torino. We saw many vineyards along the way, bought a big bottle of red wine, and passed it around as we headed back to Livorno.

The next weekend was to Pisa, and the Leaning Tower. Regrettably, I never made it to Florence.

Chapter 32

SAUDI ARABIA

Pakistani drill crew

Author

After the first briefing about my assignment in Saudi Arabia, I began to get a sense of foreboding. I learned that where I was to go, Hafur Al Batin, was a dreaded assignment. Because of its location--in the middle of nowhere--the Corps had been trying to recruit a volunteer for some time. I was to replace a Savannah District geologist named Jack Keeton. He had just gotten married a few days before he left the US, and after 3 hectic months in the desert, the Corps felt he needed some relief. The project geologist, who remained in Italy, was also from the Savannah District. His name was Charlie Canning. Directly under Charlie was a fellow geologist from Mobile--Joe Mc Reynolds, stationed in Riyadh.

The day finally came when I was to leave Italy for Saudi, accompanied by a US Army Major. We landed in Riyadh at night, in a heavy downpour, and the streets were flooded. I was welcomed to the desert by Joe and his family, and I spent the night at his villa. After more briefings the next day, I met my coworker, George Selby, from the Huntsville Division. George and I received our "tea rations" which were 5 bottles of US liquor to each of us. We were also briefed on what to do, and what not to do, concerning Arabian customs.

With Mc Reynolds leading a convoy of 5 or 6 vehicles (I was issued a full size Pontiac), we left Riyadh, traveling to Dhahran, and then north along the Arabian Gulf. When we got almost to the Kuwait border, we headed west on the Tapline highway to our jumping off point, the little village of Hafur. From there we left the highway, and navigated by compass across the roadless desert. My Pontiac was doing just fine as a desert vehicle. We passed a few landmarks. One was the "Saudi Arabian National Forest"--a lone Acacia tree!

Arriving at our destination, I saw a drill rig, a few tents, some trucks, and 3 portable buildings. My home for the next 6 months!

One of the portables was for George, another for me, and the third was to be an office. The little houses were self-contained, with all the comforts of home. We had our own water tower, diesel generator, air conditioners, flushable toilets, and complete kitchens. These buildings had just arrived, and George and I were the first to occupy them. We lived like kings compared to the other workers, who had none of these luxuries!

Chapter 33

WILDMAN JACK

When I met "Wildman" Jack Keeton, I thought he looked like a castaway from a Robert Louis Stevenson novel. Three months in the desert had taken a toll on him. He was as dark as an Arab, wild hair and beard, tattered shorts..."Are you Shaw?"..."Are you Shaw?" he shouted. "Look what I found in the desert!" he said, holding out a copper spoon. "Hey, I want to show you a sinkhole..." He was so excited to finally be leaving the place, but before he could leave, he had to overlap with me in order to show me the ropes.

The next day Jack showed me around and introduced me to the Egyptian geologist, Mohamed, and the drill crew from Pakistan. It seemed like everyone I met was named Mohamed! The workers were from many different countries, mostly middle eastern and African, so communication was a huge problem. Even the few who supposedly spoke English were very hard to understand because of the different dialects.

That afternoon, Jack and I rode to the sinkhole, which was fairly close to the camp. It was about 25 to 30 ft in diameter, and about 20 ft deep.

Jack thought there might be a cave at the bottom, and he said that he wanted to explore it before he was to leave the next day. We tied a thick rope to the bumper of his truck and dropped it over the edge. Jack grabbed the rope but then hesitated,"You know...this is crazy! I could fall and kill myself and never see my wife again!" We left without exploring the sinkhole.

The next day, a small plane landed on a dirt strip a few kilometers away at a Turkish construction camp. The Turks were building a connecting highway from the northern border to Riyadh and they shared their airstrip with us. Small planes and a ham radio were the only link we had with the outside world. Planes brought in supplies, as well as visitors from the office in Riyadh.

But anyway, "Wildman Jack", holding his copper spoon, boarded the plane, which promptly took off in a cloud of dust, headed for the international airport in Dhahran, leaving George and me to serve our six months!

Epilog: I saw Jack only once again at a geological conference in Phoenix, Arizona. He and Earl Titcomb were giving a paper there.

I retired from the Corps in 1996 and began living at my cabin on Fish River (Alabama). For exercise, I started morning walks around the neighborhood. One morning I passed another walker going the opposite direction. We spoke and kept on walking, but then we stopped and turned around. "Are you Shaw?" he said. I then recognized my old boss from Camp Leghorn, Charlie Canning, whom I had not seen since leaving Italy! I had no idea he was living in the same neighborhood.

Chapter 34

PUMPING TEST

Part 1

Drilling of the deep test well in Saudi Arabia got started soon after I arrived. The location was about 50 or so kilometers south of the Iraq border on a high gravel and sand plain. The area was empty and treeless, and unpopulated except for nomadic Bedouin tribes and their herds of goats and camels.

The purpose of the well was to test the subsurface for a possible aquifer that could supply a future Saudi Arabian air force base--the King Khalid Military City. If a suitable water supply was found, there would be many more wells drilled for an adequate supply. The drill was a big rig, the type used to drill oil wells. The derrick floor was 20ft off the ground, and the top of the mast was about 140 ft. The drillers were from the U.S., Pakistan, and Italy. The site geologists were from Pakistan and Egypt, and the crews were made up of mostly Arabs and Africans from many countries.

Communication was a big problem!

During the drilling of the well, which was to go to a depth of 5,000 to 6,000 ft, the plan was to perform a pumping test on any water zones that we encountered. The first water zone was at about 2000 ft. The crew pulled the drill stem and flushed out the heavy drilling mud. A pump was set in the well, and the water discharge was directed into a small tank. The water coming from the well was as black as oil; in fact, I thought it was oil when I first saw it. It had a terrible rotten egg odor from hydrogen sulfide. Tests showed the water was black from fossilized organic material. Although the water was not fit for drinking, the chief geologist in Riyadh--Joe McReynolds--wanted to run a pumping test.

To run such a test, the well is pumped for several hours or sometimes days. The flow in gallons per minute is measured, along with the water level in the well (drawdown). When the drawdown stabilizes, the pump is shut off and the water level is measured as it comes back up (rebound).

I don't remember how long we pumped, but it wasn't long before Bedouins started showing up at the drill rig, wanting water!

Some were on foot, some on horseback, some riding camels, and some driving Mercedes tank trucks. They formed a line and each got as much water as their containers would hold. The pump was barely keeping up with what they were taking from the tank. I couldn't believe anyone would dare drink it, but they were doing just that! I guess to a Bedouin, water is water, no matter what the purity.

When the drawdown stabilized, it was time to shut off the pump and the Pakistani geologists prepared to read the rebound. I looked at my watch and gave the signal to cut the pump off, and the water flow immediately ceased. All was quiet while the rebound and time were recorded.

After a few minutes, a stir began at the discharge tank. Then a lot of shouting in Arabic. I was sitting in my truck when a very large Bedouin came up to me, shouting and pointing to the tank. I knew what he must have been saying: He wanted the pump turned back on. I had learned a few Arabic words and said, "La, La moi"--no, no water. If we cut the pump back on, it would ruin the test, but I didn't know how to explain that to him. I got out of the truck, looking for a translator.

This Bedouin looked like he had stepped out of the movie, "Lawrence of Arabia". He was probably in his 70's with a long gray beard, a large dagger and pistol in his belt, two criss-crossed bullet belts over his shoulders, and an antique rifle in his hand--and he was getting very angry. Still shouting, he was now poking me in the chest with his fingers!

Note: Bedouin tribes were allowed by the king to carry guns. I don't know if that is the case today. JCS

Chapter 34

PUMP TEST

Part 2

By this time there were probably as many as 50 irate Bedouins around the drill rig, demanding that the well produce more water. It was evident that the situation could get violent. I don't remember by whose authority the pump was cut back on. I may have contacted Riyadh by short-wave radio (we had no telephones), but anyway, as the dirty, black water began flowing again, peace was regained, and our first pumping test was put on hold.

Water, of course, was very scarce in the desert, and the Bedouins had to depend on a few ancient wells, some dating back to Biblical times. Such a well existed a few kilometers west of our camp, and my co- worker, George Selby, and I visited this well several times. The well was in a wide and deep valley called a wadi. The floor of the wadi was green and the well was located at a "picture perfect" oasis, complete with desert palms. We watched some Bedouins drawing water. There was a wooden pulley, a goatskin bucket, and a lot of rope to retrieve the water, which was at a very deep level. The rope and bucket were lowered by hand. When the bucket filled, the rope was tied to a donkey, which pulled the heavy bucket back to the surface.

This procedure took a long time and many trips in and out of the well to get enough water. I felt sorry for the poor donkey. No wonder they were so excited to get water from a motorized pump like the one in our well!

Chapter 35

STEALING ARAB WOMEN!

Toward the end of my tour in Saudi, the size of our camp had grown considerably. Instead of a handful of workers, we now had hundreds. The Pakistani drill crew and drill rig had been replaced by American drillers and a drill rig large enough to drill an oil well, albeit we were hoping to hit water, not oil. The American drillers were a rough and extremely bigoted bunch, and treated the Arabs and Africans terribly. The camp boss, a hardnosed Texan, had to be watched like a hawk to make sure he stuck to the government contract. He knew that George and I could shut down the whole operation if we saw any infractions, and we did just that a few times. He got mad at me because I would not allow him to dump the camp garbage in the sinkhole, mentioned in the last chapter.

There were three separate dinning rooms--strictly segregated-- one for Whites, one for Arabs, and one for Africans. Partly, the reason for this was because of the different food preferences. Whites ate Australian beef and potatoes, Arabs ate goat and lamb, and Africans ate mostly vegetables. I got so tired of steak and potatoes every night that I started eating with the Arabs and Pakistanis. They seemed to appreciate my presence, especially since, by then; I was able to speak some Arabic.

For several weeks, Bedouin nomads were camped nearby. On several occasions, while driving across the desert in my Pontiac, they would wave and motion to stop. I decided to try out my Arabic and pulled up to one of their camps. I greeted them in Arabic, and they treated me like a special guest. I was led to a black tent and sat down on a rug lined with pillows. The men soon had a fire going in a sand pit, using something like sagebrush for fuel. Out came a large brass coffee pot, and within a few minutes, I was drinking some of the worst coffee ever brewed--called gawah. It would have been impolite to refuse it, and I knew I was supposed to drink at least 2 cups. Thank goodness they were small cups! The second course was some camel milk from a wooden bowl. I had read that Bedouins like to flavor it with camel urine! But they insisted that I try it, so I took a sip as they passed it around. When it was my turn for a second sip, it was more than I could bear. I jumped up, ran out of the tent, and threw up. When I finally looked back, the men were roaring with laughter.

On many occasions, I would drive to the small village of Hafur, about 50 kilometers north of our camp, to buy vegetables and fresh fruit. George and I had started using our kitchens to cook for ourselves. On one such trip, I was traveling alone in a pickup. I passed an Arab man and woman walking, and the man asked for a ride. He got in the passenger side, and made the woman get in the truck bed. He pulled out a cigarette kit and began rolling a smoke. After he lit it, I realized it was marijuana. The woman kept looking through the window and smiling. She was not veiled. When we finally arrived in Hafur, I understood enough to know that he was trying to sell me the woman. I bought tomatoes and oranges instead!

One day some Bedouins stopped by our office and invited George, myself, and two other Corps personnel to come to their camp that night for a 'goat grab'--goat or lamb roasted on a skewer over a wood fire. We accepted and drove over that night. The whole goat, including head and legs, were cooked. We sat on a Persian rug under a brilliant star filled sky. The women brought out some oranges. Most of the time the women stayed hidden, but were peeking out from a separate tent. They were covered from head to toe, except for their eyes. The meat was delicious, and I was offered one of the eyeballs, which is considered an honor! However, I faked eating it, and stuck it under a pile of rice when no one was looking.

The next day we decided to take some candy over to the Bedouin's camp, to show our appreciation for the delicious meal. When we drove up to the tent, we didn't see anyone. After a few minutes some children appeared and beckoned us to come inside. We gave them the candy and they were all smiles. We noticed that there were some women in the back tent, but they didn't come out. Finally, we left and headed back to our camp. As we drove along, we noticed one of the Bedouin men walking in the distance. He was waving at us, so we drove over to him. Immediately, we realized that he was very angry. He was shouting in Arabic and began hitting our vehicle with his hands. I thought he was going to break the windshield! Luckily, we had an engineer with us from Sudan who spoke Arabic. From their exchange, the Bedouin seemed to really become enraged, so we drove off. We learned that he was mad at us because he had seen us coming from his camp, and he thought we were going after his women. I think there was probably some discipline in his camp that night. I made sure the door to my house was securely locked for as long as they remained in our area. Bedouin tribes were allowed to carry guns, and they all had long daggers in their belts!

Chapter 36

MONTH AT SEA

Part 1

In the Spring of 1987, I spent an entire month aboard a drilling vessel that was taking cores from the Continental Shelf off the coast of west Florida. This was a foundation investigation for the U.S. Air Force. Eight borings were drilled into the sea floor for future radar towers, at various locations from the Florida Panhandle to the Florida Keys. The vessel, R.L. Perkins, was a converted supply vessel, approximately 250 ft. in length, with living quarters for 2 drill crews, a crew of scientists and engineers, and the ship's crew. The ship was leased by McClelland Engineering in Houston, Texas, which also furnished the drill crews and technical personnel for the U.S. Government contract. I was on board strictly as a Government Representative (the only one on board). My job was to see that the drilling was done according to the contract and to sign off on the GPS (Global Positioning System) coordinates. In other words, the location of each boring had to be within a 30 ft. tolerance of the chart location. A surveyor was sent to operate the GPS system, which at the time, was very new technology.

I boarded the ship on April 9, 1987, relieving John McFadyen, a fellow Corps geologist. He had acted as a Gov. Rep. during drilling in the northern Gulf of Mexico. Now it was my turn. The ship left the dock in Pascagoula, Mississippi, just after midnight. At a top speed of 10 knots, we arrived off the coast of Ft. Myers on April 11 for our first boring in 105 ft. of water. The clarity of the Gulf was astounding! The sea floor was easily visible, and it was a treat to see the curious dolphins that came over to see what we were up to.

The first boring did not go well. The drill stem became stuck and broke off, leaving 20 ft. of pipe sticking up from the sea floor. The captain, Floyd Beau, said there was a Florida law that no man-made objects could be left on the bottom that would hang up fishing nets, so he called for a diving team out of Ft. Meyers. When they arrived, they quickly went down and severed the pipe with a type of explosive.

The second boring was off Dry Tortugas Island, where the old prison stands that held Dr. Samuel Mudd (he doctored Boothe) after the War Between the States.

Since I didn't have much to do, I got bored after a few days, and joined the off duty drill crews at fishing. Every morning, there were plenty of flying fish on deck for bait. In the clear water, we were seeing some large fish hanging around the bottom of the ship. They were barracuda, and we were hooking them right and left! However, we never got one up to the surface because, when they were hooked, they always dove under the sharp edge of the ship's bottom and broke the line.

There was a day shift and a night shift, but during bad weather and rough seas, we could not drill. One storm lasted for 4 days. I slept in a top bunk in the bow, so I got the maximum pitch of the ship's motion, but never got sick. I wore a patch for the first few days. Food was ok. We ate at a large table, 3 meals a day. At night, I would go out on deck and watch the drilling. There was always a poker game in the rec room, but the stakes were too high for me. Alcohol was strictly forbidden at sea. I drank a lot of Kool Aid! There was a video player with some movies, and a small library.

Every day or so I had to call the Mobile office on the ship's radio and report in to my boss, Roger Johnson. The captain and crew laughed when I talked over the radio, because I was always saying, "That's a Roger...Roger", or "Roger that...Roger", or "Roger Wilco...uh, Roger".

After the call I would say, "Well, it's hard to talk to someone named Roger over a 2-way radio!"
"Roger that!" said the captain.

To be continued...

Chapter 36

MONTH AT SEA

Part 2

I don't know what kept the old R.L. Perkins afloat! Being a drilling ship, a large portion of the bilge was filled with liquid drilling mud, which is very heavy and dense. That caused the ship to sit very low in the water. At times, depending on the "mud load", the freeboard was only a foot or two above the water. Seas would sometimes wash clear across that part of the ship, especially when underway. It was a wonder no one was lost overboard.

Migratory birds were a common sight. Many different species would land on the ship for a much needed rest. I saw the occasional Magnificent Frigate bird, flying over the ship. A Chuck-Will's-Widow (look it up!) was perched on the anchor chain for two days. It would periodically drop down to the water for a while, and then fly back up to the very same spot on the chain. There were all sorts of warblers. I feared for them, because the little things were walking all around where the men were working. I'm sure some of them were killed, either from heavy drill pipe crashing down, or the men accidentally stepping on them. They would not, or could not, fly to get out of the way! I would go up to the high bridge deck and just sit up there, while warblers would be walking around on my arms and legs...even my head. I would kill flies with a fly swatter and feed them as they sat in my hand! They were so hungry!

They stayed a few days, and then one morning they were all gone.

After about two weeks out, we had a major problem. The ship's freezer went on the blink. The crew could not repair it, and they had to dump all the frozen food in the sea. The captain refused to go into a port to have it repaired, so we had to eat mostly canned food. The cook did what he could to make meals more appetizing, but there was only so much he could do. Fishing went from sport fishing to survival, but we had very little luck. Someone got the idea of throwing a small cast net at night to catch squid, which were everywhere. This worked and we were treated to calamari dinners.

When we ran out of Kool Aid, that was the last straw! After the threat of mutiny, Captain Floyd headed the ship into Port Manatee, just off Tampa Bay, for groceries...and Kool Aid!

My time aboard was drawing near as we set up on the last remaining boring. That night as the drill crew began sampling, we were hit by a major storm. I was in my bunk and the motion was so bad, I thought I would be slung against the ceiling. I could hear banging, clanging, and shouting from outside, but I just stayed below, and finally drifted off to sleep. When I awoke and went out on deck, the place was a wreck! The ship had been rocking so badly during the storm that all the drill pipe had been bent up like a corkscrew. With no tools to drill, that was the end of the drilling, and, for me, the end of the voyage.

The captain radioed for a "taxi" boat to come to the ship to take me into Ft. Myers. From there, I would fly back to Mobile. The 25-mile ride in that little "taxi" boat was fast, but rough. For the first time in a month at sea, I got seasick!

Chapter 37
HONDURAS (FIRST TRIP)

Part 1

I went on two assignments to Honduras for the Corps. The most recent trip was in 1991.

The first trip was sometime in the late 80's.

First trip: The primary purpose of that trip was to advise U.S. Army and Honduran Army personnel on water well drilling, and to test for the presence of ground water near a Honduran Army camp.

The flight out of Houston was on a Honduran commercial airliner. The jet was a 'hand-me-down' and probably should have been grounded years ago, evident from the many cracks in the windows, the dirty seats, and the torn carpet. However, they served the very best meal that I have ever had on a plane...plus excellent wine. We were not scheduled to land in Tegucigalpa, but for some reason we landed there before going on to San Pedro Sula. The man sitting next to me started cursing when he found out we were landing in Tegucigalpa, because he knew it had one of the most dangerous airports in the world. I saw what he meant when the plane had to make a steep bank between two mountains, just miss some high power lines, and then dive onto the short runway, and hit the brakes, hoping to stop before going off a steep cliff at the other end! "Honduran pilots!...Best in the world!" said the man, as he finished his wine.

In San Pedro Sula, I met a Honduran Army officer, who was to drive me along the north coast to the old picturesque town of Trujillo, which was near the camp. We left the next morning. The ride was the most hair-raising trip I have ever made in a car! This officer drove like he was in the Talladega 500, on a narrow, winding road, with steep drop offs, and no guardrails. Honduran peasants dry coffee beans on the warm pavement, sometimes taking up half the road. On several occasions, we had to suddenly swerve around beans and peasants, missing by just inches! I tried to slow him down, but I realized that was the way they all drove. Like the Honduran pilots, they are also excellent drivers.

After a delicious seafood lunch in La Ceiba, we finally arrived in Trujillo. Our destination for the night was an old hotel (The Beverly), located on a high hill overlooking Trujillo Bay. There was only one vacancy, so I had to share a double room with "Lead foot". When I awoke, he was in the bathroom, and I noticed a.45 automatic under his pillow! I was glad he was leaving.

That morning I took him to catch a small plane back to San Pedro Sula, leaving me the rental car. My second contact was an American Army captain, and we went to the Honduran Army camp to discuss well drilling.

That night, the hotel had some new arrivals. They were some sort of "spy type" officials with the U.S. Government (one was a woman). They invited me to join them for drinks and dinner on the veranda. We all had the special--Honduran lobster and ceviche, with all the other delicious tidbits (it would be worth going back there just to have that meal again!).

At the time, there was some anti-American guerilla activity in Honduras, and when we went into the countryside, six Honduran soldiers accompanied us. They were teens with M-16's, and were very eager to use them. We arrived at a U.S. Army camp high in the mountains, where a well was being drilled for a water supply. I met with the drill crew. They told me that the night before, some thieves had been shot, trying to steal some of the drilling equipment. Also, there were some snipers in the area. Sniper bullets had hit an Army caravan, but luckily, no one had been hurt. I later learned that was the reason for the "spies" presence.

Chapter 37

HONDURAS (FIRST TRIP)

Part 2

That night the captain and I stayed at the U.S. Army camp, which was overlooking the Aguan Valley in northern Honduras. We were assigned to one of the tents, which were about 15 ft. square, with a plywood floor. There were about 6 or 8 other men in our tent. The modern Army does not segregate. Male and female enlistees were assigned to the same tent, and the mix looked about 50-50. Modesty was not a concern. They dressed and undressed in mixed company. The shower tent, however, was separated (male and female) with a sheet of canvas hanging from the middle of the tent. Urinals were out in the open, and were 4" sections of pvc pipe, stuck into the ground at a 45-degree angle, at crotch height. The toilets were more private, enclosed plywood outhouses. I say "private"...some were "one-holers" and some were cozy "multi-holers".

Until the well was finished, water was supplied by a reverse osmosis pump, which pumped water from a muddy stream nearby. The process furnished clean potable water, but it took a while to get sufficient water for the whole camp.

After an almost sleepless night (someone was sawing and hammering during the night!), the captain and I met with the drill crew again, wished them luck with the well and bid them farewell. We rounded up our 6 Honduran bodyguards (they had hoped to shoot some more thieves) and headed back for Trujillo... and another delicious lobster dinner at the Hotel Beverly.

A terrible thing happened the next morning. A young Honduran man walked into the hotel lobby, bleeding profusely. His arm had been nearly severed in a machete fight, and he wanted someone to take him to the hospital. The captain volunteered and put the poor man in the bed of his pickup truck, and drove into town. I didn't know about all this until the captain got back. There was blood all over his truck bed, and he was washing it with a hose. The doctor told him that machete fights were very common in Trujillo.

We both checked out of the hotel later that morning. The captain left for another army camp. I left in the rental car to return to San Pedro Sula, and for a flight back to the U.S. the next day.

On the way back (I was traveling alone), I got lost in El Progreso which was a hot spot for anti-American gangs, I saw graffiti saying "Gringo Go Home" on some adobe walls. I had a map but the roads were not well marked. I stopped at a little store in town to ask directions. The man at the counter was grinning from ear to ear when I walked in with the map. He knew I was a lost "Gringo". He could speak no English but pointed to an intersection, saying "San Pedro Sula...Si, Si"

I made it back to the Hotel Copan in San Pedro Sula late that afternoon...headed for the bar and, later, one more 4 star meal.

Chapter 38

BIG ISLAND, ARKANSAS

Back in the fall of '89, the Corps sent me on an assignment to take a drill crew into a remote area of northeastern Arkansas.

Driller Charlie Brown and I were to hire local help (2 men) as crew. The job was to drill a water well for an aquifer test at a future lock site on the bank of the White River. The site was one of the most inaccessible locations I had ever worked in, and was called "Big Island"-- a large tract of land between the White, Arkansas, and Mississippi rivers. It was like a jungle with thousands of acres of huge trees, thick underbrush, vines, muddy swamps, and gullies. There were a few trails but no roads that we could drive a truck mounted drill rig on.

The area was leased for hunting deer, but all we saw were a few wild hogs. We had been warned to look out for "booby traps" set by people who occasionally farmed small patches of marijuana. Thankfully, we never encountered any.

We hired two local yokels (one black and one white) from the little town of Dumas, Arkansas, where Charlie and I stayed. The town was about 25 miles from the site. For an entire month, the work consisted of hacking out a road to the lock site. We were also slowed by frequent storm fronts.

When we finally got to the drill site, the helpers, who of course were very inexperienced, had to be shown every move, and Charlie was getting impatient with them. One day, as they were trying to unscrew a drill rod, Charlie told the white helper to hit the rod with a hammer to loosen the joint. Instead of hitting the rod, he missed and hit Charlie on the hand. After a string of cuss words, Charlie fired the guy on the spot!

Charlie had yelled, "You're a fired sonofabitch! Go over there and stay out of the G--D-- way!" But Charlie hired him back after a few minutes since we needed all the help we could get--even if it was green. After that episode and a few others-- the helper was fired and hired several times--the two just did not get along. So the white helper, whose name was Steve Oswald, began riding with me to and from the job while the other helper rode with Charlie.

One day Steve said that he was kin to Lee Harvey Oswald, the one who shot President Kennedy. I doubted this at first, but he seemed to know so much about his uncle and how they were related, that I started to wonder if it might be true. The other helper (I don't remember his name) was very quiet and did what he was told. He was a Vietnam vet, and Steve was very wary of him. I found out why as we rode to the job. According to Steve, who was much younger, the vet was telling him war stories about Vietnam and was obsessed with the killing that he had seen over there. Steve said that the guy kept telling him how easy it would be to "take him out" and would go into great detail how he would do it!

I was not surprised when both of these guys were soon in trouble with the local police. Steve was arrested for DUI but came back to work for a while. The vet was arrested on some sort of domestic violence, and we never saw him again. A new helper (Tommy Cooper from the Corps) soon arrived.

Chapter 39

TUNICA

While on the Arkansas job, I drove up to Memphis, Tennessee to get some supplies from Carloss Well Supply. On the way back, my government Suburban broke down near Tunica, Mississippi. Tunica was a very small town about 30 miles south of Memphis, located in the flat Mississippi Delta near the river. The population was mostly Black and cotton farming was the major industry.

Luckily, I pulled in to a Chevy dealer just before my truck totally expired. It was about 5 pm, and they were getting ready to close. The manager said they could have my truck repaired by some time the next day. I asked about a motel nearby, and he said there was only one motel in town but that he would not recommend it. I knew I had no choice so they got an employee to drop me off at the Tunica Inn. The place was a real dump--a line of tarpaper-covered shacks and no pavement--just gravel and dirt. The "office" was in a house on a hill nearby. The owners were from India. I got a room and opened the door. A pungent odor greeted me, and I realized they probably rented these rooms by the hour! The bed took up almost the entire room with a small TV in front. There was a single window and one of the panes was cardboard. The bathroom was tiled and there was a live tree frog in the tub. Home sweet home!

After returning from a cafe down the road, I settled in for the night. I watched TV until about 11 pm and turned in--not under the cover but on top. I dozed off only to be awakened by a lot of loud voices, doors slamming, cars running, and all kinds of disturbing racket. It was now about 1 am and the place was really getting lively. There was no use trying to sleep, but I eventually did doze off again. Soon, a loud rapping on my door reawakened me. I looked outside through the curtain and saw a large black man standing outside. I didn't make a sound or open the door, and after a few more raps, he went away. Now I was really wide-awake.

At 3am--more knocking! I got up and peeked out. There were two black men at my door and a third in an older model Cadillac--engine running! I wondered what in the world these guys could want with me? I could picture myself robbed, tied up, and stashed in the trunk for a short ride to the dark waters of the Mississippi. This time, they kept on knocking so I decided to escape through the bathroom window. I opened the window and looked down. It was a vertical drop straight into a deep gully. No escape that way! When I went back I saw the doorknob turning and I looked around for a weapon. I pulled out my Swiss Army knife, which had a 3-inch blade, dulled from years of logging core. I should mention that there was no phone in the room to call for help.

Then the knocking sounded further away. They were at the room next door...and then further...they were going on down the line, knocking on doors.

I sat there on the bed until the sun came up, and when it did, I slept. At sometime that morning, I was awakened by a loud knock. It was the cleaning woman saying it was time to check out--10 am. And check out I did. I told the manager at the office about all the ruckus, and he said that the men were looking for their sister whom they suspected was with a man in one of the rooms. But the manager would not give them the room number, and that was why they were knocking on all the doors. If they found them that night, I can only guess what happened to the man with their sister!

After a leisurely breakfast at the town cafe, I picked up my truck and never wanted to see Tunica again! Ironically, since casino gambling was legalized in Mississippi, Tunica is now like a Las Vegas of the South, a vacation spot with big name entertainers and multimillion-dollar casinos and hotels. I don't know if the Tunica Inn is still there, but if it is, I hope they have paved the parking lot, and put phones in the rooms.

Chapter 40

THE FOSSIL

Back in the 80's I attended a Corps Geophysics class in Dayton, Ohio. It lasted about 5 days and on one day we took a field trip to a limestone quarry. I picked up an interesting 'L' shaped rock that was full of brachiopod fossils. When the class was over, I decided I would try to bring it back with me on the plane. So I put it in a large, manila, government envelope and sealed it up. I had no problem getting through security, and carried it under my arm as I boarded.

After we were airborne, a man in the seat next to me asked what was in the envelope (it was heavy and bulging). I didn't tell him...I just picked up the envelope and handed it to him. I said, "What do you think it is?" He felt of the package for a few seconds and said, "I know exactly what it is! It's a.45 automatic!" I never told him what it really was. I put the envelope back under the seat, and that man never said another word to me for the rest of the trip. It's a wonder I wasn't arrested!

I doubt if the security people would have known what it was even if they had examined it! JCS

Chapter 41
NEW YORK CITY, 1990

Drill crew--Passaic River Project, N.J.

One of the most interesting TDY assignments that the Corps sent me to was New York City. At first, when my boss in Mobile, Roger Johnson, told me where I was going and for how long (5 months), I thought NYC was the very last place I wanted to be. I was sure I would probably be gunned down by the Mafia!

I was to work with the New York District as a field geologist on the Passaic River Flood Control Project, which was located in New Jersey, just across the Hudson. The project had been on the books for a number of years, and the Corps had finally gotten some Congressional funds to do a geologic study, using Mobile District drilling crews.

The Passaic River floods a high density population of eastern New Jersey every so many years, and the project was to construct a 40 ft. diameter flood tunnel below the river from its headwaters to its outflow into the ocean (Newark Bay). During times of flood, several huge vertical shafts would be opened, and floodwater would be "dropped" into the underground tunnel, eliminating a disastrous and costly flood. This project was so huge (billions of dollars), that the Corps decided to form a separate division: the Passaic River Division with a main office in Hoboken, N.J.

The plan was to have 3 TBMs (tunnel boring machines) cut through 40 to 50 miles of basalt rock, which was about 50 to 100 ft below the ground surface. The TBMs were to be left in the ground in side tunnels because retrieving them would be more costly than what the machines were worth. The drilling was extremely difficult because of what lay on top of the basalt--several feet of glacial till. Till is an accumulation of granite boulders of all sizes, left over from the last Ice Age. It took skilled drillers like Charlie Brown days to get through the till and set casing into the basalt so that coring could begin.

But before any drilling was done, there were many weeks of office work at the New York Federal Building in Lower Manhattan, where the Corps occupied 3 floors.

I arrived in NYC for the first time in my life during mid February and got a room in the Roosevelt Hotel on 47th St. On my first week end, and after learning how to use the subway system, I saw the sites: the Statue of Liberty, World Trade Towers, Empire State Building, South Street Sea Port, etc. On St. Patrick's Day I got up early and walked across town a ways and had a late breakfast. Big mistake! I knew about the parade but when I left the restaurant to go back to the hotel the avenue was blocked and the parade had already started. Even though my hotel was just a few blocks away, I was not allowed to cross the street--for hours and hours. So I had to watch the whole parade.

Chapter 42

NYC "CAESAR SALAD"

My main job at the New York office was trying to secure drilling permits on private property along the proposed tunnel route.

Russell Acheson, a geological engineer, with the NY District, was overseeing that procedure. A few weeks after my arrival, the Mobile office sent a newly hired female geologist named Laura Waite. She was sent up to help with the permitting, and to get some field experience with the drill crews and me. Laura had studied at the University of London, finishing at the University of South Alabama with a B.S. in geology. She was extremely smart and efficient, so it didn't take long for her to be a real asset to the project, as well as greatly improving the "scenery" in the office. Laura didn't like the old antiquated Hotel Roosevelt and moved to the Dumont Hotel on 34th St. It was new and had kitchen facilities in each room. At about this time (April), I returned to Mobile for 2 weeks leave.

When I returned to NY, I also moved into the Dumont. One weekend a couple of Laura's female friends that she had known for several years came to visit. It was "Earth Day", and they invited me to go with them to Central Park where there was music and eco-talks by eco-folks. One of the speakers was Christopher Reeve (Superman).

On another occasion, a young female engineer (I think her name was Jill) in the office asked me if I would like to go to dinner with her in Greenwich Village that night. I was sort of surprised that she asked me since I had just met her, and I was old enough to be her father! Anyway, I said yes, and she told me the name of the restaurant and when to meet there.

After getting off the subway, it was raining but I found the restaurant, and Jill was in the lobby. There was a waiting line so we registered and got in line. We each had a menu. As we talked and studied the menus, I noticed Jill was sort of leaning against the wall.

All of a sudden she said, "I think I'm going to have a seizure."

"Yeah, that sounds great! I think I'll have one too!" I replied. "I love caesars."

"NO! I'm having an epileptic seizure! Not a Caesar salad!" she explained, as she started to slump down the side of the wall, her eyes rolling to the back of her head.

I was horrified. "Wait! Wait!...Don't do this!" I was saying, trying desperately to hold her up against the wall. And then as quickly as it came on, she regained her composure and said, "OK...It's over. I'm sorry but I get those seizures every once in a while. I never know how long they're going to last or when they're going to happen".

Well, she recovered nicely and we had a nice dinner. She said that her father was a medical doctor.

And although I wanted one, I did not order a Caesar!!

Chapter 43

NYC "ON THE STREET"

The Corps per diem rate for New York City was so high, that I could use my week end per diem to buy round trip air fare to Mobile just about every week end. So Laura and I would check out of the hotel on Friday, take a cab to La Guardia, and be in Mobile that evening, returning Sunday afternoon.

One Sunday night, as we returned to the Dumont, I had forgotten to make reservations and the hotel was full. Laura had her room, but I had to take a cab across town to another hotel in a less desirable part of town.

From that area, I had to get up a little earlier to catch the subway, and the station was run down, dark, and spooky. One early morning, as I walked to the stairway leading down to the trains, I noticed a black man crouching down behind a dumpster. When I got to the stairs and started down into the darkness, he came out from behind the dumpster and followed me.

He got up real close and said, "HEY, you goin' to work?"

I had been warned about street people and muggers--to try to ignore them and to not say anything if they ask something.

Man: "Hey, you goin' to work man?"

I glanced back but said nothing. He then got right up to my ear and said in a quiet voice, "You better talk to me, man!"
With that, I turned around and said pretty loudly, "YEAH, I'm goin' to work!" But when I turned, my foot slipped and I fell a short way down the steps, dropping my briefcase. I was sure I was going to be mugged, stabbed, or worse when I felt the man's hands grabbing me! But instead, he was helping me up! He picked up my briefcase, handed it to me and said, "Man, you be careful now, ya hear".

I thanked him and walked on through the turnstile on the other side of the station and awaited the train. It was probably 10 or 15 minutes until it arrived, but during those long minutes, the black man was staring at me. He was about 20 feet or so away, and I tried not to stare back. But he never took his eyes off me until I stepped onto the train. I honestly think he had planned to mug me that morning, but when I slipped and fell, he actually felt sorry for me and changed his mind! Who knows, he might have been a mental case. There were certainly lots of them around. Shortly thereafter, I moved back to the Dumont.

In 1990 homeless people and panhandlers were everywhere in Manhattan, especially around Grand Central Station. I learned very quickly not to buy anything from the little shops in there, because when the clerk handed back your change, there would be 3 or 4 other sets of hands trying to snatch it! The smell of urine was strong in all the subways. I remember walking along Park Avenue one bright sunny Saturday, and noticed a young homeless man sitting on the top step of a bank building. I couldn't believe what I was seeing. His pants were down to his ankles, and he was doing his morning 'business' right there on the steps, totally oblivious to the hordes of people walking along the sidewalk.

Another time, as I was waiting to cross a street, a man standing next to me hollered as loud as he could, turned and hit the wall of a stone building with his fist! You could hear the bones crack...I left!

I don't know why these things happen to me, but there was another time when Laura, Russell, and myself were walking back from Lower Manhattan, I noticed a large homeless man wearing an old beat up Army jacket, unshaven, and dingy looking (picture Nick Nolte), picking up something from the gutter. As we walked toward him, he started staring at us with a vacant look. I was walking on the outside, and as I walked by, he drew back and took an exaggerated swing at me! Luckily, I ducked and he almost hit Laura, but missed both of us. We kept walking and he just kept standing there in the gutter.

JCS

Chapter 44

NYC "Movie Debut"

While in New York, I saw several movie scenes being filmed. All of the scenes were on the street. Some of the actors, I didn't recognize. I saw a blond actress being filmed as she was carrying a bunch of packages. That could have been some advertisement.

One afternoon, as I was walking around a corner I was stopped by a film crew filming a scene. A bus was parked near the curb and I recognized Matt Dillon, not James Arness, but the younger actor. They were filming him as he stepped on the bus. There was no dialog, just him walking up to the bus and stepping on. As I stood there and watched, they filmed that over and over again with the director yelling "Cut!" each time. Why, I don't know. How hard is it to step on a bus!
I could have done that scene!

On another afternoon, I left the Corps office heading for the subway. It was raining slightly, and I saw a film crew shooting a scene on the side of the street. This time the director wanted people to be in the film as passersby, but I just stood back to see what the scene was about. There were two actors, a young, pretty female and a big tall man. I didn't recognize either of them. The scene was them hugging and then a long kiss. I didn't know it at the time, but that was the final scene of the movie.

On the second take of that scene, I decided to walk by and get in the scene. There were several cameras--one to film the "passersby" people--me included. Every time they did a "take", I walked by, back and forth, back and forth. I was sure that I had to be in at least one shoot.

Anyway, I found out that the name of the movie was "Green Card" and that the actress was Andy MacDowell. The man was a French actor.

A year later I rented the movie that I was sure I was in! But they cut my scene! The film editor probably said, "Who is that idiot that keeps walking back and forth? We'll have to use the first take. I don't see him in that one!"

Chapter 45

NYC "FINAL WEEKS"

When I stayed in the Roosevelt Hotel, I noticed two very innovative homeless men. Just across from the main entrance, they had set up their "home" in a double doorway that was inset so they were shielded from the wind. The doorway was boarded up so it was no longer in use. On the concrete floor was a small steam vent, over which they had erected a clear plastic tarp, and the rising warm air from the steam vent kept the plastic tarp blown up like a balloon. Inside, they had their bedding on top of cardboard mattresses. During warm days, they would just remove the "roof" and move over to the other side of the doorway where there was no steam vent. For food, they would crawl through a dumpster near a deli where they retrieved discarded food. I'm sure they must have panhandled for a little change, probably for necessities such as wine and tobacco.

Back to the job in New Jersey: When the permitting was done for the drill sites, some of the Mobile drill crews began arriving in their trucks and drill rigs. Several borings were drilled and tested.

However, the drilling was soon halted by the state of New Jersey's Environmental Protection Agency, because the Mobile drillers were not licensed in that state. The NY District sent Laura and me to the EPA office in Trenton to take the written test to become certified New Jersey "well drillers".

The Mobile District has the world's best core drillers, but they had a hard time passing the written test. Laura and I passed it, so although we were certainly not qualified to actually operate a drill rig, we signed off as the "drillers" to satisfy the NJEPA.

When June arrived, my TDY was just about over. Mobile was sending me on another job. Laura was to stay on and continue working with the drill crews.

Before I left, the NY office gave a "going away party" for Russell Acheson, who was quitting the Corps in order to go back home to Wheat Ridge, Colorado, to assist with his ailing father. He had a geological engineering degree from the Colorado School of Mines, but became a paint salesman at a Lowes store. He was the most dedicated and capable engineer in the whole office, so he was sorely missed.

Epilog: The Passaic River Flood Control Project was going to cost as much or more than the Tennessee-Tombigbee Project. Like all huge water projects, it was very political. There were high-level meetings, Congressional hearings, etc. But after a few years of study, Congress rejected the whole project as too costly and construction of the tunnel was never begun.

During my 28 years with the Corps of Engineers, I worked on many "studies" of projects that never came to fruition. Some of these studies took years and millions of dollars, such as the Sea Level Panama Canal and the Cross Florida Barge Canal, which were never built.

Also, studied to death but never built, were the many missile silos to be located all over the US (Project MIRV under Nixon), a nuclear waste repository in Kansas, the "Star Wars" Laser experiments at White Sands, NM (Reagan), restart of a nuclear reactor at the Savannah River Plant, and many dam and lock sites--all had geological and engineering studies but were never funded for various reasons. However, the controversial Tennessee-Tombigbee Waterway, which I worked on for 10 years, was one Corps project that was completed, even though it narrowly escaped environmental lawsuits and the Congressional axe. JCS

Chapter 46

HONDURAS (2ND TRIP)

Part 1

In 1991 I was sent to Honduras again. The purpose of this trip was the same as the last: to assist a U.S. Army camp and Honduran villages in the Aguan Valley, find potable water by drilling wells.

I arrived in Tegucigalpa on Feb. 28, and was met by a U.S. Sergeant. We flew from there by helicopter to the Honduran/U.S. Air Base, Soto Cano. I thought I would be staying there for the night, but after supper, the Sergeant said, "Mr. Shaw, it's time to go to Camp MaCora." MaCora was 150 miles away! He drove me to a dark airstrip and we waited for my transportation. It wasn't long before I heard a chopper coming. The Blackhawk helicopter landed and I got on with my bag. There were no lights inside or out, and I felt my way to a seat and buckled up. We lifted off but hovered only about 5 ft. off the ground for 10 or 15 minutes. I later learned that was standard procedure to test the critical oil pressure.

After we got up to our cruising altitude, which was about as high as a Blackhawk could fly, I learned that U.S. helicopters had recently been shot at, and that was the reason we were flying at night, with no running lights or cabin lights. The flight took about 2 hours, and looking down, I saw many small fires in the forest below. Peasant farmers were burning small patches of the forest to clear land for subsistence crops.

We landed after 10 PM and I was ready to bed down anywhere (I had been flying all day). The first person I met out of the chopper was the commanding officer, Lt. Col. Brooks. He said, "Are you Shaw?... come on to my tent for a meeting about our well drilling". He was so excited to see me. He seemed to think I was some sort of a "wizard" that was going to solve all their water needs! I didn't even know where I was...much less where to find some water! I tried to sound intelligent, but by midnight, I'm sure I was babbling incoherently from lack of sleep.

Camp MaCora was in a mountainous area of northeastern Honduras. The U.S. Army was building a road through the mountains. A special unit was there to drill the wells. They were the 200th Red Horse Unit of the U.S. Air Guard. They had a truck mounted drill rig, a type that I was familiar with.

After a MRE (meal ready to eat) breakfast, I left with a convoy of Hummers to proceed into the Aguan Valley to meet with the "presidente" of a small village.

At the village, the whole townsfolk showed up to meet us. They were so excited and enthusiastic. I didn't speak Spanish, so I had two Army translators. When the 'prez' showed up we all gathered 'round...

men, women, and children...all smiling! Typically, they wanted their well drilled in a convenient spot like a park or near a public building, but it was up to me alone, the "Great Water Wizard", to make the decision where to drill!

Some of the places where they wanted wells, I knew would not produce a drop of water, because of the type of rock, and the lay of the land. I really didn't have much to go on--no geologic map, no prior knowledge of the area (I had been in the Aguan Valley before but in a different part).
But I had to spot the well somewhere, so I took a hammer and a stake, walked over to what I thought was a likely spot, hammered the stake in the ground, tied a ribbon to it...and said, "Drill Here!"...and everyone cheered!

The same scene was repeated in 7 more villages, always with a large crowd of curious and happy onlookers. All I did was spot the well locations. The actual drilling of the wells was done weeks later...after I was safely back in the U.S.

Were they successful? I don't know. I hope so!

Chapter 46

HONDURAS (2ND TRIP)

Part 2

On my last day at Camp MaCora, the drill crew brought in a tub of iced-downed beer for all the members of our tent...we each got 2 beers. While we were finishing our refreshments, there was a sudden volley of small arms fire from where the road crew was working. This caused an all out alert and soldiers were grabbing their weapons and running toward the perimeter gate. The drill crew and I stayed behind. We were not combat personnel.

We heard no more shooting. Apparently, no one was hurt. The snipers ran back into the forest. A dump truck had turned over during the fracas, and the focus afterwards was to right the truck.

The next day, 2 huge Chinook helicopters landed at the camp. One was my ticket out of there. I bid farewell to Col. Brooks and the drill crew and walked up the ramp of the chopper. Both choppers were to fly back to Soto Cano that afternoon. Ours was to carry a big generator, suspended from a heavy strap, so the cargo door had to stay open during the flight. We took off and the second Chinook followed. After a few minutes in the air, the following Chinook went down. It had lost oil pressure and had to make an emergency landing. We circled back and, seeing that they were safely on the ground, we went on. I guess they had radioed the camp for help(?)

Anyway, our chopper made it to Soto Cano Air Base, where I spent the night in one of the barracks... in a real bed.

I left for Tegucigalpa the next day in one of the strangest aircraft I have ever been on. It looked like a "cartoon" plane...a very fat fuselage, a tall tail, 2 small propellers, and, except for the cockpit, no windows. The plane was loaded with passengers, all in rows of seats like a conventional commercial plane...but no windows whatsoever (I guess the cartoonist forgot to draw them in!). I was glad it was a short flight, because it was very warm in there (no A/C), and I was getting claustrophobic.

March 4:   Arrived back in the U.S.
        No problems.

JCS

Chapter 47

SAVANNAH RIVER PLANT

The Savannah River Plant near Aiken, S.C. is a US Government nuclear materials processing center, encompassing thousands of acres along the Savannah River. It was built in the '50s for the purpose of producing radioactive material such as Plutonium and Tritium for nuclear weapons. I guess it still serves that purpose today.

In the early '90s, I was sent there to work with the supervising government contractor, Westinghouse, and the DOE, who were planning to restart a small nuclear reactor that produced Tritium. Tritium is a radioactive "trigger" used to detonate a Hydrogen bomb. Tritium has a half-life of just a few years, so it has to be remade ever so often in order to periodically "re-arm" nuclear weapons.

What was my assignment? Well, the DOE was concerned that the foundation under the reactor might have shifted, and they wanted me to take a small crew of laborers and technicians to look for, and verify, any evidence of that. A trench around one side of the building had already been dug with a backhoe. The plan was for laborers to dig out with shovels (the foundation was sand) a layer at a time, under one side of the reactor floor. Then I would go in and look for any bedding displacement, indicating movement. I would photograph and describe the layer in a log report.

Security: I should mention that restarting the reactor was an utmost priority for the Pentagon, because at that time, the Tritium supply in the U.S. was very low. There was an extreme sense of urgency to get the foundation problem (if there was one) solved, so that the reactor could start producing more Tritium. Wackenhut was the agency in charge of security, so before I could even think about going to the site, there was an entire week of security briefings, badges, and classes on the dangers of radiation.

A week later, I was ready to go to the reactor site with the crew. This involved passing through 3 levels of security (the last level was a finger print scanner). There were 4 of us from the Corps, and each of us was assigned to a DOE "buddy". While on site, your buddy had to keep you in sight at all times, even when using the restroom! We had to wear dosimeters (radiation detectors), and do 3 urine tests per day, to test for radiation in our bodies. The reason for that was because we were working very close to "hot" cooling water pipes. In fact, to get under the reactor floor, we had to crawl directly over them. At the end of the work day, we had to pass back through the security levels and then step into a full body scanner before we were allowed to leave the plant. I was staying in a motel in Augusta, Georgia, about 30 minutes away.

This went on for a couple of months, reporting what I saw and photographed, to the Westinghouse boss every other day. One week he (boss) took my photos and logs to Washington D.C. for a Congressional Hearing. I don't remember there being any major problems with what I saw of the foundation.

When the Westinghouse boss (I don't remember his name...Dr. ?) returned from D.C., my Corps boss, Roger Johnson, wanted me to come back to the Mobile office, and go on a different assignment. I was thrilled to be getting away from such hazardous duty.

When I reported to Westinghouse, I told them that my boss was pulling me out. "Oh no, he's not. You're not going anywhere!", said they. I got Roger on the phone and he was adamant that I get in my truck and come in. I then passed the phone to my other boss, and they had a heated conversation: "No, he's not leaving. This job takes priority..."

When I got back to the motel, I didn't know whether to leave the next morning for Mobile or not. And then, later that evening, I got a call. It was Roger Johnson. He said he had just been called by someone at the Pentagon! Roger had been over-ruled. I had to stay and finish the job. It was a matter of national security!

It took another month before I finally got out of that place... and many more months before I stopped glowing in the dark!

JCS

Chapter 48

NO RELIEF!

My worst nightmare happened to me while I was on a geological assignment at the Savannah River Plant near Aiken, South Carolina sometime in the early 90's. I was staying in Augusta, Georgia, which was not too far away.

One evening I was looking forward to some seafood at the local Red Lobster in Albany. When I arrived, the restaurant was packed. People were sitting around in the waiting lobby, so I went into the rest room to use the facilities. As I walked in, I noticed a short, dumpy old guy with a veteran's cap washing up. I was at the urinal to get relief. I really needed to go!

All of a sudden the old vet starts whistling...and it was loud! He walked over to stand behind me, still whistling this tune.

This made me uneasy and I could not go.

"Do you know what that was", he said.

"Pardon me?"

"That tune I was whistling. You know what it was?"

"No! What?" I was still trying to go.

"COLORS", he shouted. "That's what a bugler plays when there's no band. It's the same as the National Anthem".

"That right?" I said, zipping up...I gave up trying to go.

"BERNARD SWARTZ--HUN'ERD AND FIRST AIRBORN!" He was still shouting. "I was with Patton in the 'Big One'...Dubya Dubya Twooo! Yep. He had them two pearl handled pistols ya know...like in the movie".

All I could think of is why doesn't this guy leave? I'm dying in here! Yet, he goes on telling me his war stories, so I decided to go back out to the lobby. He followed!

In the lobby, all the benches were occupied, Swartz and I had to stand. I was hoping he was with someone and would go join them, but no--the horror of horrors--he was alone.

Swartz: "Hey, you need any life insurance? Here's my card. I sell insurance". This was even worse than war stories. Now he was trying to sell me insurance!! Now, I'm really dying. Finally, they had a table for me.

"Nice talkin' to ya" said Swartz, holding out his hand. "yeah, me too", I lied. But when he shook my hand, he would not let go! He was squeezing my hand like a hydraulic vice, while at the same time, trying to 'Indian wrestle' me!!"

"Pretty good for an ole man, eh?", he said.

"Yeah, pretty good", said I, finally wrenching my hand loose and running for my table. As soon as I ordered, I dashed back to the rest room. This time, no one was in there, but I was not taking any chances. I went into the stall and closed the door. Thank God...no whistling...no war stories...just relief ! True story.

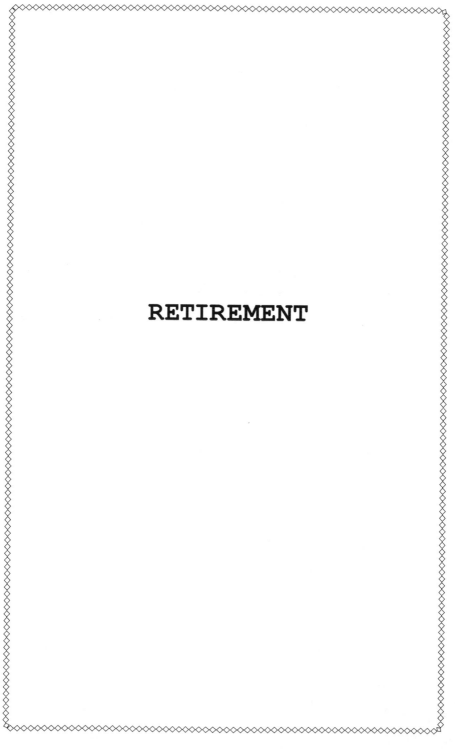

RETIREMENT

Chapter 49

EARLY OUT

During the mid 1990's the Corps of Engineers was ordered to downsize and began offering early retirement to a number of employees in the Mobile District, which was, and still is, one of the Corps' largest districts. I was stuck in a dead end slot with no chance of advancement, and decided to ask for an early out. The Corps was also offering an incentive bonus of $25,000. So as a GS-11 (top step) and 28 years service, I retired on January 3, 1996 at age 52. Also retiring at the same time were quite a few core drillers that I had worked with for many years.

After buying a $26,000 sailboat, I was preparing for the easy life on the Alabama coast where I owned a waterfront cabin on Fish River. The boat was a used Pacific Seacraft Flicka trucked in from Key Largo. It had gone through Hurricane Andrew but was in good shape. Although a Flicka is only 24 ft. long (including bowsprit), it is rated as an ocean cruiser with a sizable cabin, standing headroom, head, and a small diesel engine.

On a cold January morning, the boat was rigged and launched at a marina in Fairhope. I sailed alone down the east side of Mobile Bay into Weeks Bay and up Fish River to my pier, a total of about 20 miles. I have been a sailor most of my life, buying and selling about 10 different sailboats. One was destroyed during Hurricane Frederick in 1979.

I had bought my waterfront lot and new cabin (700 sq. ft.) in 1973 for $18,000 which, at the time, I thought was a very high price. Now, of course, that sounds like a bargain. Another wise purchase that I had made in 1972 was a cabin near Taos, New Mexico in the Sangre de Cristo Mountains for $16,000. It has always been a wonderful and cool place to escape to for a few weeks during the unbearably hot Alabama summers.

After three months of retirement, I found myself employed again. This time with a grouting firm based in Houston, Texas. Also onboard were three of my co-workers from the Corps who had retired at the same time I did--Herman Scott, John Bush, and Doug Jones. They were employed as drillers and I as the field geologist. The job was near Mineral Wells, Texas at the site of an existing reservoir-- the Palo Pinto Dam. The right abutment wall of the dam had been displaced a few feet by torrential rains, and the plan was to set tension anchors to a rock base in order to realign the wall.

During the second month, Herman Scott was involved in a serious accident. The folding derrick on the drill rig suddenly came crashing down, landing on Scott's forearm. His arm was crushed and badly broken. 911 was called and he was flown by helicopter to a Dallas Hospital.

The drill rig was a rental and it was determined that a steel pin which secured the derrick was not supplied by the rental company. Without this pin, the derrick had failed. This resulted in a lawsuit between Scott and the rental company months later.

As a witness, I had to give a deposition for Scott's attorney, but I think the case was settled out of court.

In the meantime Scott's injuries were treated and he went back home to Alabama to recouperate.

My job was to log the core and see that the anchors were set firmly into rock. I stayed on until the last boring was done in early June. The next job was to be somewhere in Montana, but I decided that I wanted to get back to retirement, so I resigned and headed back to Alabama. Two weeks later, I was at my New Mexico cabin for the summer.

Although I have had several offers, including re-employment on Corps jobs, I have not been employed since the job in Mineral Wells (1996).

Chapter 50
MAGGIE

Casting off for a sail (Maggie in the bow)

Ready for the walk

Maggie the dog found me--not the other way around. When I retired, I had no intention of getting any kind of a pet, but nevertheless, I was adopted. It happened one day as I was sailing along the river in a small dingy, just enjoying the light breeze, when I noticed a strange white dog swimming out to my barely moving boat. The dog caught up with the boat and was trying to get in! I kept her out because if she had gotten aboard, I would have capsized. I kept seeing the same dog in our island subdivision every day...a very thin, scraggly looking stray that looked to be about one year old. Her hair was mostly white, but sparse. I thought she looked something like a coyote. None of the neighbors claimed her, but she took up with a neighbor's dog named Ghost, who was a white chow that belonged to the Schambeaus down the street. The little Schambeau girls gave Maggie her name.

Maggie was a survivor! She was cunning and mischievous at the same time. She ate whatever she could find... dead fish, garbage, and stole food from other dogs' bowls, especially Ghost's bowl. Mr. Schambeau was getting ready to take Maggie to the pound. "That's the worst piece of dog flesh on this planet!" he told me.

In the meantime, Maggie had been sleeping on my porch and brought me a "present" every morning. She would steal my neighbor's belongings and bring them to me...shoes of all kinds, socks, jackets, bathing suits, sheets, skates, a bag of ant poison, workmen's lunches, even people's underwear! On halloween she dragged in a scarecrow that someone had put up as a decoration! I was horrified because I had no idea whose stuff it was. Well, I found out later that a lot of it belonged to the Schambeaus and I returned it to them. That's when I learned that they were going to take her to the pound. I had already started to bond with Maggie. I was feeding her at night, and she would follow me on my morning walks. So I told Mr. Schambeau not to put her in the pound, and that I would take her as my dog.

But Maggie continued to be a problem. Not only did she continue to steal, but she was very vicious toward other dogs in the neighborhood. One evening she came home with two pellet gun wounds...undoubtedly from a neighbor. She loved people but she would attack any dog (except Ghost) for no reason at all. She sent at least four dogs to the vet. That prompted a visit from the county animal control who warned me about her running loose. Thus, a $2000 fence was put up; however, she soon learned to get through the gate.

As Maggie grew older, she became a very pretty dog with thick white fur and a bushy white tail.

She watched me like a hawk, not letting me out of her sight. She would chase after my truck until I would have to stop and let her in. She learned my habits and knew what I was going to do before I knew myself! If I wore a certain pair of shoes, she knew whether I was going walking or going to town. If I took a shower or shaved, she would run out through the dog door and wait at the truck, because she knew I was leaving.

Much to my dismay, she and her pal Ghost took a toll on the local wildlife, such as muskrats, possums, rats, rabbits, young birds, even snakes. Together, they would surround a tree that had a squirrel, and bark and confuse the poor squirrel until it would finally take a suicide leap, right into Maggie's jaws.

To control Maggie, I bought a cap gun and some caps. If she started to do something that I didn't want her to do, like chasing another dog, I would shoot the cap gun, and she would immediately come cowering back. After leaving her behind on my annual summer trips to Taos, my neighbor who fed her said that she would get so depressed that she would not eat. So I began taking her with me in the truck each summer--2600 miles round trip. On one trip, we had stopped to get gas, and Maggie jumped out of the truck and was running all around the place. I was calling her but she ignored me, so I got the cap gun. I should say that the cap gun looked very real. So there I was, walking around a busy truckstop with a gun in my hand! People were looking at me like I was going to rob the place, so I quickly stuck it in my shirt, which looked even more suspicious. Luckily, Maggie came back to the truck without me firing a single shot. We got out of there fast, in case someone was calling 911!

Maggie loved the water and loved to go sailing with me in the small dinghy. I built a carpeted deck seat in the bow, and she learned to move to the windward side whenever I tacked. Many times, boats slowed down to take our photo.

At this writing Maggie is at least 14 years old. She has arthritis now and has really slowed down. We still walk every morning. She insists! She can no longer jump into the truck, so I built her a foot stool. Just recently, I learned the reason for her eccentric behavior all these years. She is not really a dog, but an Arctic wolf, or at least bred from one. When she was younger, she would howl on occasion! I learned of her wolf breed from talking to people that had the same species. One owner, I met at the vet, had a beautiful male wolf...just like Maggie but younger and much larger. And he was barking at all the other dogs and being obnoxious... just like Maggie!

With all her faults, Maggie has been my beloved companion throughout most of my retirement years here on Fish River, and I intend to keep her going as long as possible.

Chapter 51

WADDLES

In July 1997 hurricane Danny hit the Gulf coast. It was only a category 1 but it was the storm that wouldn't go away! It stayed around the eastern shore of Mobile Bay for about a week, dumping tons of rain. The Weather Channel showed video of many houses on upper Fish River entirely under water. At one point it even got over the Hwy. 32 bridge which normally is about 25 ft. above the river. I live on the lower end of Fish River, so by the time the flood waters got to me, it was only a couple of feet deep in my yard.

A few days after the storm, I noticed something white on the boat ramp next door. It was a Mandarin duck, pecking at a water-logged loaf of white bread. He was so weak he could not break the plastic wrapping, so I cut it open, and he immediately started gobbling the soggy meal--probably the first meal he had eaten since the storm. He was a fully grown duck. His wings had been clipped so he could not fly. After a few days, he quickly recouperated, and I fed him white bread every day. He would not touch whole wheat. It had to be white bread! He got pretty tame and just hung around my waterfront and pier area for months. I finally had to build a little gate with a sign that read "No Ducks" in order to keep the duck poop off the pier. My neighbor, Katy Foster, who had her mailbox on my pier (our mail is delivered by boat) named the duck "Waddles".

With the arrival of fall, Waddles' wings had grown back and he started trying to fly. He could get airborne for about 20 feet or so, but after much practice, he flew all the way across the river and back. Over the next few weeks, he would fly into my yard and waddle up to my deck, wanting some white bread. I would throw out a few pieces and off he would go. This continued for a while, and eventually he quit making his visits.

During the spring of the next year, my dog Maggie and I were taking our daily canoe ride when I spied Waddles swimming along at the end of a quiet bayou--and he had a wife!--also a Mandarin.

Over the next year or so, Waddles flew into my yard one more time. He was alone. Having no white bread, I rushed to the store and bought some, but when I got back, he was gone. That was the last time I saw Waddles.

The "No Ducks" gate was still on my pier until Katrina swept it away in 2005. Until then, It served another purpose: keeping Maggie the dog from biting Huey the mailman!

Chapter 52

WILD NIGHT

"Hell's Swamp" is an extensive cypress swamp in north Mobile County, and is one of the last habitats for Black Bear in Alabama. Locals call it haunted because sometimes at night you can see the eerie glow of marsh gas dancing through the mist. And "Hell's Swamp" was almost my last destination on this planet.

On a Sunday night (Dec. 2005), family members and I were invited for supper at my sister's brother in law's home which is on the edge of the swamp. We had a nice meal and afterwards, Bill was showing the menfolk his gun collection, while the women sat by the fire in the den. Bill opened his gun safe which was in his office (he is a forester), and pulled out a deer rifle. Before handing it to Chris (a non hunter and my niece's husband), Bill said "When you pick up a gun, the first thing you want to do is check to see if its unloaded." Chris took the rifle, checked the breech, and after seeing it was unloaded, clicked the trigger. This was repeated several times with different rifles.

I was not paying much attention to the "gun show", just walking around in the room looking at stuff when BOOM!!...the rifle fired and missed my head by inches! The bullet went through a double pane window and out across the front yard. Everyone in the room was just staring in disbelief. "How could an unloaded rifle fire?" we were all thinking. Bill's wife Peggy was out in the yard walking the dog and heard the shot as well as the others in the den. Of course when they found out what had happened, they were horrified. Thank goodness the only casualty was the window pane. We left shortly thereafter and rode back to my sister's home in Daphne--sobered and shakened!

When I got back to Fish River at around 10:30, I was shocked to see a large paramedic ambulance in my driveway. There were flood lights around my pier-- firemen, paramedics, and marine police--all stirring around near the water's edge. I walked down to see what was going on and saw blood on my pier, a wrecked jetboat tied to it, and another boat up in the marsh weeds nearby. There had been an accident during the Fish River Christmas parade. Apparently, the boat in my weeds was a parade boat, and had collided with an oncoming jetboat. The three people in the jetboat were from the Marlow Volunteer Fire Department. One was a young woman in critical condition. She was flown by helicopter to the hospital just before I arrived at the scene. It was her blood that was on my pier where the paramedics had administered CPR. The rescuers worked late into the night pulling the two wrecked boats out of the river, using my boat ramp. I finally went to bed around midnight. It had been a wild night!

The next day as I was returning from grocery shopping, I saw a Channel 5 news team in my driveway. Reporter Debbie Williams asked if they could interview me and take some video of my pier and the accident scene. I couldn't tell them much since I was not home when the accident occurred, but they interviewed me anyway.

Sadly, the young woman fireman died in the hospital a few days later. The volunteer fire station in Marlow was later named for her.

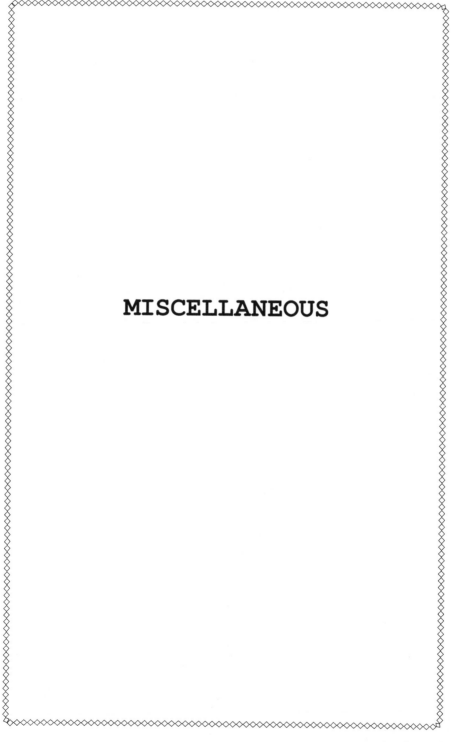

MISCELLANEOUS

Chapter 53

HYPNOTISM

Meditation? It's sort of like being hypnotized isn't it? The most vivid feeling I have had of being in this mental "zone" was at a Turkish contractor's camp in Saudi Arabia. Their camp was a few kilometers north of our location, and the Corps shared a small dirt air strip with them. George Selby and I got to know them pretty well, and they would sometimes invite us up for a meal.

On one occasion, the boss Turk had his whole family there at the camp, and we had a nice lunch with them. Afterwards, we were all just sitting around, and the boss Turk wanted to play a Merl Haggard song on his player to see if we could tell him some words in the song that none of them could understand. The song, "Proud to be an Oakie from Muscogee", was a big hit and I had heard it many times. Anyway, the lyrics that they were wondering about were: "We still wave 'Ole Glory' down at the courthouse, and white lightnin' is still the biggest thrill of all". They said, "What means this 'oh glory' and this 'white lightnin'? We Americans who were there (Corps people) thought this was pretty funny, and realized that these Turkish people, although they could speak English very well, didn't have a clue as to the meaning of Merl Haggard's folksy lyrics.

But, back to the subject of hypnosis. After explaining the words in the song, the boss Turk asked me if I would like to play chess with his young daughter who was about grammar school age. I said that I would, and we sat down at a small table in front of a big fan. I don't remember the little girl saying anything, but as I sat there and watched her set up the chess men on the board, I actually went into a hypnotic state. It was quiet, the fan was running, and I instantly felt a sense of total calmness that is hard to describe. A bomb could have gone off, and I would not have cared the least bit! I know that sounds crazy, but I think I was actually hypnotized. I remained almost euphoric and totally relaxed all afternoon and did not come out of it until dinner that night.

I don't know what triggers this state of mind, but it has happened to me a few other times...maybe less than half a dozen times.

I can remember a time in Tennessee, while visiting a historic Indian village, I had the exact same feeling, but it did not last as long. That episode was triggered by the mere sound of a man's voice, a total stranger who was talking to me about the park when I was instantly "zoned"! Another time, while getting my palm read (also in Saudi)...the same thing.

It would be nice to be able to enter this mental state at will, since it is such a euphoric state. I wonder if it is the same feeling as meditation?

When I told this story to some friends, they said that those Turks probably slipped a "mickey" in my kool-aid!

Chapter 54

LONDON TRIP

It was sometime back in the 1980's that I took a trip to London. My sister, Suzanne, was going over there to reunite with her husband, Malcolm, for a short vacation, and I decided to tag along. Malcolm, a civil engineer, was permanently stationed in Saudi Arabia with Stone and Webster Engineering, and was periodically given short R&R vacations to various locations...usually in Europe.

Anyway, our flight descended on an early morning into a thick London fog and managed to find one of the runways at Heathrow. We never saw the ground but were greatly relieved to be on it!

We met Malcolm at the Savoy Hotel where he and my sister had reservations. I stayed a few blocks over in the Covent Garden area at a small, less expensive hotel. For much of that week, we went our separate ways.

Being a sailing nut, I went to a huge boatshow in Kensington, and on the next day, took a tour boat down to Greenwich to see the "prime meridian" (zero longitude) and also the National Maritime

Museum. The next day I took a train to Portsmouth to see the HMS Victory, the flagship of Admiral Horatio Nelson. I was surprised to see that it still existed, since it was launched in 1765 and was in the Battle of Trafalgar. It was in a dry dock and is still a registered ship of the British Navy! The tour inside the ship was excellent. Afterward, I toured an exhibit nearby where archaeologists were in the process of preserving one of King Henry VIII's ships.

Then it was on to a waterfront watering hole for a pint or two.

When I returned to London, I rejoined Mal and Suzanne and we saw a play that night--Les Miserables--which we really enjoyed. Mal wanted to stay a little longer than planned, but the Savoy was booked, so they had to move across the street to another hotel--the Strand. I helped them move and afterward, toured around alone. It was early afternoon and I was looking for a good restaurant for our evening meal. Just up the street, I found an interesting looking Italian restaurant. It was beginning to rain so I headed back to my hotel in the Garden district. When I rejoined Mal and Suzanne that night, it was raining cats and dogs. We decided to try the little Italian place that I had seen that afternoon, so we struck out in the pouring rain. We got soaked, even though it was a fairly short walk to the restaurant, but we made it inside and got a table. We ordered drinks and dried out as best we could. After a great meal, Mal said he would be right back. He was going to the front desk to see if he could buy some cigarettes. When he came back he was grinning like a cheshire cat! "Do you know where we are?", he said. "We are in the Strand Hotel!"

When he went to buy cigarettes, they had directed him down a hall, and was shocked to find himself in the lobby of the hotel where they were staying. Here we had slopped through the pouring rain and gotten soaked when all we had to do was walk a few steps from the elevator. Mal never let me live that down! For years, he loved to tell that story..."and old Craig said, 'Hey, man, I found this great little Italian restaurant and it's not too far from your hotel...'"

Chapter 55

THE MOONING

These days we've all witnessed road rage and it's usually an unpleasant experience. However, this story involves road rage that I still laugh about.

You had to know Valda Wright to really appreciate the humor in this. She was the mother in law of my sister, Suzanne Wright. Valda died a few years ago and the South lost one of its best cooks of truly "southern" cuisine. She was a pillar of the Dauphin Way Baptist Church, a retired school teacher, and loved to tell stories about her younger days, growing up in Kentucky.

One late Sunday afternoon I was driving Valda back to her home in Mobile. We had been enjoying a family meal at her son's home in Daphne, Alabama. She was sitting in the front seat of my pickup, telling me a story about the wonderful garden her mother grew in Kentucky, and was naming all the different vegetables.

The traffic was unusually heavy on the Bayway, and I was trying to give some interest to her story when I noticed something happening in the rear view mirror. A white Mercedes occupied by a distinguished looking couple was trying to pass a convertible (top down) occupied by three college aged students. When the Mercedes pulled out to pass, the convertible swerved over to prevent the Mercedes from passing. This went on for several miles and each time, the Mercedes was blocked by the convertible. I could see that the man driving the Mercedes was getting very angry, turning red in the face and shaking his finger at them. The young man in the rear seat of the convertible was looking back and laughing.

As we approached the George Wallace Tunnel, Valda, oblivious to what was going on outside, was still telling her story..."Mama Kenzie grew some of the most beautiful tomatoes!..."

When we entered the entrance to the tunnel, the couple in the white Mercedes were in the left lane but still behind the college kids. As both cars came around us, the kid in the back stood up and pulled down his britches and underwear, "mooning" the irate couple behind them. I don't know the outcome of that "road rage duel", but if the man driving the white Mercedes had some sort of a anger stroke, I would not have been surprised. Both cars sped on ahead, leaving us far behind.

What was really amusing to me was that I realized that Valda had no clue of what had just occurred. She never saw a thing and I didn't tell her. She was lost in a time warp, somewhere near Bowling Green... in a vegetable garden..."Oh, those tomatoes!"
JCS

Chapter 56

UNCLE WICK

I have never been a spender. I have always saved money. I think it's in my blood. Most of my relatives on my father's side were the same way. Not that they were misers (well, a few might have been), but they held on to their money. I had four bachelor uncles--great uncles--who, when they died, left a relatively large some of money. One uncle, Wick Fox, was a hermit who lived on 1800 acres of family land, a mixture of forest and pasture, in rural Marengo County, Alabama.

With a small pension from the railroad, he retired to a broken down, unpainted shack at the end of a long winding trail (I wouldn't call it a road). He had a few cows, chickens, turkeys, guinea hens, and no electricity until his sisters, my Aunt Sue Connor and Aunt Lucretia Hawkins, insisted on his getting an REA line. There was an outhouse and a hand dug cistern, said to be dug before the Civil War. An old black woman named Bessie would come and cook for my uncle, and she would sometimes stay in a back room of the house. We called her "Aunt Bessie" and she was a wonderful cook. During the summer, she would pick wild plums and make a delicious plum jelly--and also plum wine. She said that her mother was born during the slave era.

Uncle Wick's house was like a share croppers' shack, built off the ground with rough boards, a rusty tin roof, and a rickety old front porch. The yard was dirt with a huge pecan tree in front. Inside, the walls were papered with newspaper, and there were two fireplaces made of "slave brick". In the kitchen was a cast iron wood burning stove, and next to it was a new electric stove--again, at his sisters' insistance--but it was never even installed.

Uncle Wick did not own a car and for transportation, depended on catching a ride out on the highway. He would occasionally visit his sisters and brothers who lived in Uniontown, Alabama, which is in Perry County.

His attire was quite unique. He was a small man, usually dressed in overalls, size 4 brogans, a pith helmet, and walked with a stick. He always had a cigar and wore cheap reading glasses that still had the price label stuck to one of the lenses. His disposition was jovial and he had a comical way of speaking--an "Old South" accent, with a bit of an Irish twang. He had fought in World War One and was cited for bravery as a "runner" behind enemy lines.

Although he had only a grammar school education, he was quite intelligent. He liked to read and became somewhat of an accountant, doing income taxes for some of his rural neighbors.

Uncle Wick lived to a ripe old age, quite content, a simple hermit-like existence, until he finally died alone. He was found some time later, after no one had seen or heard from him in a while.

In 2001, the 1800 acres was sold to Weyerhaeuser for over two million dollars.

Chapter 57

Everyone has a Story

Everyone has a story, whether good, bad, funny, or sad, it's just a matter of searching your brain for memories. Time will eventually rob us of our memories if they are not written down, and then they are lost forever.

I never intended to write a book. In fact most of these stories were merely e-mails to a friend who saved them on her computer, and who encouraged me to keep writing. After writing quite a few stories about my career with the Corps, I decided to make it sort of an autobiography, including memories of childhood through college, and on into retirement. At least it would be of interest to family and friends, and would serve as a record of my existence after I am gone.

For other readers, if my stories drew a laugh or a smile, or tweaked a memory of timely events over the past half century, then I feel satisfied that I took the time to reflect and record.

John Craig Shaw